HAND PAINTED TEXTILES
FOR THE HOME

HAND PAINTED TEXTILES
FOR THE HOME

KAZZ BALL
AND
VALERIE JANITCH

David & Charles

To Stephen, Charlotte and Joshua

(frontispiece)

FLOWERS IN CERAMIC. A black gutta outliner and glowing colours give this lovely painting the sensation of sunlight captured in stained glass. Worked on Habotai silk with Deka-Silk paints, this piece is particularly interesting because it employs several other techniques to create unusual effects.

Coarse salt was sprinkled over the wet paint to simulate an artistic 'glaze' on the ceramic pot. Salt was also used on the azure background, but when the first application of silk paint was dry, the background was painted again with slightly diluted Deka-Permanent paint in the same colour, leaving wide flat brush strokes which give the silk a completely different texture

British Library Cataloguing in Publication Data
Ball, Kazz
   Hand painted textiles for the home.
   1. Decorative arts. Textiles
   I. Title   II. Janitch, Valerie
   746

ISBN 0–7153–9400–2 Hardback
ISBN 0–7153–0157–8 Paperback

Designs © Kazz Ball, 1991
Text © Valerie Janitch and Kazz Ball, 1991

Illustrations on pages 67, 69, 91, 103, 122, 129, 147 and 151 by Alison Hoblyn
Photographs on pages 9, 35, 36/7, 47, 53, 59, 61, 63, 81, 85, 87, 101, 105, 107, 108, 119, 125, 131, 133, 141 and 143 by Di Lewis
Photographs on pages 15, 16, 23, 50/51, 112/113, 135, 137 and 139 by Alan Duns

Typeset by ABM Typographics Ltd, Hull
and printed in Singapore by Saik Wah Press Pte Ltd
for David & Charles plc
Brunel House Newton Abbot Devon

First published 1991
Reprinted in paperback, 1993, 1994

 # INTRODUCTION

I had been involved in textiles and needlecraft long before I first set eyes on a piece of hand-painted cloth, but as soon as I was introduced to fabric painting I saw its fascinating possibilities.

In a short time, fabric painting has become recognised as one of the most popular new art forms. It can be enjoyed as a hobby or used for many practical purposes, without previous experience. In this book, I have sought to compile a whole range of original and colourful examples of hand-painted projects that you can work on in your own home, and I have tried to explain them in step-by-step instructions that are easy to follow. The possibilities are endless once you have acquired a minimum of skill. There are so many ways in which you can brighten up the interior of your home, and so many uses to which fabric painting can be applied. It is my hope that this book will encourage readers to participate in a whole new world of activity.

I was born, bred and educated in the Netherlands, so English is only my second language. I could never have expressed myself so clearly without the invaluable help of Valerie Janitch, an enthusiast for fabric painting, who has helped me to put this book together. I am very grateful to her.

Kazz Ball

My own enthusiasm for fabric painting was aroused when I first saw Kazz Ball's work. It was like hearing a vibrantly exciting piece of music for the first time.

I saw the fascinating results achieved when Kazz combined her wonderful colour sense with the glowing textile paints to perform ridiculously simple techniques, like dabbing the paint on with a sponge or – still more fun – sprinkling it with salt and watching a magical pattern appear . . . Then I suddenly wanted to find out how other methods might be simplified in the same way: so that they could be understood and successfully attempted by anyone who, like me, would love to 'have a go'. Hence this book: the words are mainly mine – but the music and the inspiration are all pure Kazz!

Valerie Janitch

CONTENTS

CHAPTER 1

DESIGN AND INSPIRATION FOR PAINTING

Before you start to paint, you must of course decide what your subject is to be, and how you are going to paint it. There is nothing wrong with basing your work on existing textile design. Artists have been learning from other artists since time began, and *whatever* you do is sure to be influenced by something you have seen and liked, whether you are conscious of it or not. But the thrill of seeing your very own unique design hanging across your window or cushioned in a chair is heady stuff indeed; the creative satisfaction is immeasurable.

There is no need to panic at the thought of trying to 'do-it-yourself'; if you're imagining you need to be an artist to create your own designs, you couldn't be more mistaken. But once you begin, you may be surprised to find you have hidden artistic talents you never suspected!

All you need are ideas and inspiration. And, contrary to what you may think, these are not hard to come by – if you know where to find them. Where to look? All around you! From your garden to the greengrocer, from pets to pottery, from fashion to your freezer, from magazines to children's books. It's all there, waiting for you to see and use it. All you need to do is gather up all the material which excites *you*, and put it together in a 'source book' so that you can study it and allow it to influence your ideas and suggest your subjects. This part can be almost as exciting as the painting itself!

COMPILING YOUR SOURCE BOOK

First you will need a ring binder and a large plain pad to fit it: a lined pad is useful too, for written notes. Apart from a pen and pencil, have a paper glue stick or a tube of glue, and some suitable pins and tape with which to mount your specimens. Felt pens or crayons are useful to remind yourself of colour combinations, but a small paintbox, which allows you to mix shades much more accurately, is even better. Always carry a small sketchbook with you to jog your memory when something takes your eye: a few lines and a scribbled note will usually suffice to remind you, and if necessary, you can expand it later, when you have more time. And of course, where circumstances permit, a camera will capture a permanent record in seconds.

Your source book will become a collection of all the things which you have found to inspire you. As it fills with sketches, photographs, fabric samples, magazine clippings and colouring ideas, you will have a treasure trove of creative design sources at your fingertips. Apart from stimulating your creative talents, it will also help you to reap the benefit of the experiment and experience of other designers: so watch out for new ideas and applications.

As soon as you begin to search for inspiration

The source book – an invaluable repository of exciting ideas

you will find that the subjects you can choose from are infinite: you can go anywhere, turn in any direction, and if you look, you will see. Collect and hoard any ideas which you personally find eye-catching. Even such things as labels which impress you with their design or striking combination of colours. For example, many cosmetics and toiletries come attractively packaged with sophisticated designs in subtle shades: whilst others will appear equally stylish through the clever use of bold, primary colours.

WHERE TO LOOK

A walk in the country, or just around your garden, will supply a whole portfolio of inspiration. Try to be alone and let your mind wander. It's difficult to do this if you are distracted by your partner, children or even an energetic dog. Don't hurry: there's so much you might miss. As you stroll along, study the shapes of leaves: willow, ivy, oak. Pick good specimens of the ones you like and press them between sheets of blotting paper to mount in your source book. Think of them at different seasons of the year. Imagine the fresh yellow-green of the willow as it first greets the spring . . . and picture the pale leaves falling across a drift of white muslin: see the dark green ivy leaves against plain cotton the intense blue of a midsummer sky: or crisp brown oak leaves clustered on shimmering gold silk.

Study the colours and detailed patterns of bark, noting how much each variety of tree differs from the rest. Search for nuts, fruits, berries and seeds amongst the leaves. Have you ever looked at the colour scheme of a crab-apple? That exciting combination of bright green, orange and red would look wonderful painted on pure white cotton for a child's room.

Or if there *are* no leaves, the black tracery of bare branches makes a stunning pattern, soot black against a monotone sky, whether it is a clear, cold blue or leaden with imminent snow: or most dramatic of all, against the burning brilliance of a winter sunset. Study the way the trunk of the tree divides into a few thick branches – which divide into more, thinner branches – which divide into thick twigs – dividing into thinner twigs – and so on . . . With this in your mind, and your fabric as the sky, you certainly don't have to be an artist to cover it with bare branches: it's no more than

doodling with a paintbrush.

Watch out for birds and animals, too. Not just the creature as a whole, but pick up fallen feathers . . . they can be long and straight and sturdy like a quill pen – or small and round and fluffy like eiderdown: both can give you ideas for painting. Sheep grazing in a field could be translated into very simple black and white shapes on a green ground; chirpy round bright yellow chicks might be hopping over a rich red-brown background, suggested by their mother's glossy feathers; a cluster of delicate blue-green eggs would contrast with the surrounding dull brown tones of their nest, if viewed from above. Or scan the sky for distant birds soaring and wheeling against the clouds, as stark a contrast as the bare branches of trees in winter.

DON'T MISS ANYTHING!

Notice *where* you are walking, too. Stone paths bordered by a brick wall, perhaps. Try to count how many colours, and shades of colour, you can see in a brick wall. The older it is, the more you will find. The same goes for stone walls, of course, where you may have plants and flowers, moss or fungi growing between the stones, adding even more interesting contrasts. The shapes of flagstones, or the geometric arrangement of a brick path, the symmetrical lines of a wooden fence or a curved stone bridge over a stream: think of them all in terms of pattern and colour, and how with brush and paint you could reproduce them in the form of a fabric design.

Out in open country, stop to admire the wonderful shades of gold which have inspired so many artists, as the breeze ripples through a field of ripe grain. And try to imagine the old days,

This delightful cushion shows how a simple motif can be very effective when techniques and materials are complementary. The swallows and gold cage were painted onto Habotai silk using the gutta-serti technique (see pattern overleaf). The painted panel was backed with cotton and a thin layer of wadding, then the painted design was outlined by handstitching, to give a quilted effect. The finished panel was then set into a cushion cover

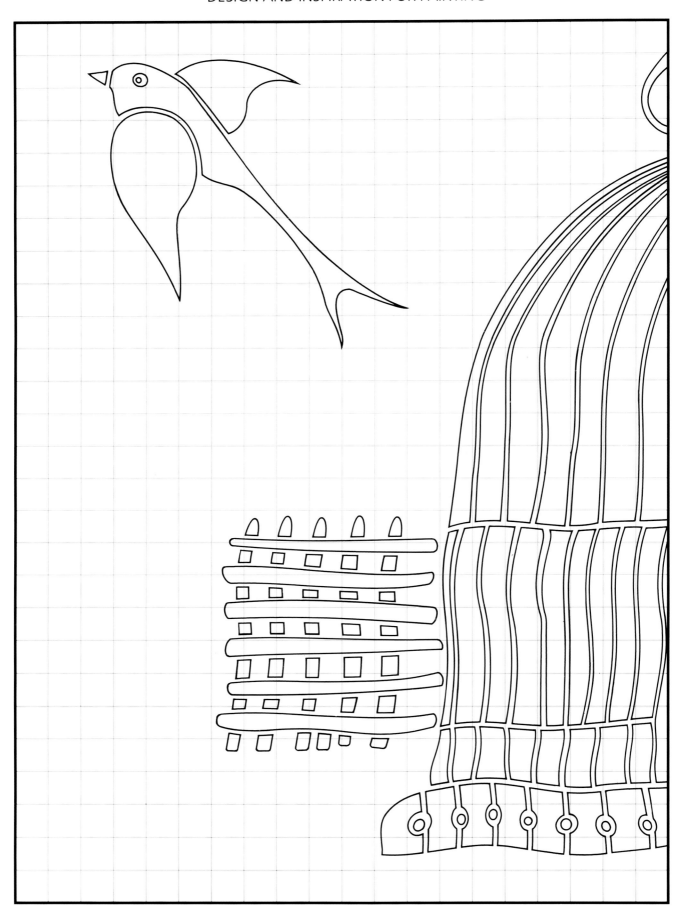

when vivid red poppies and bright blue cornflowers grew in the cornfields. Then visit your local library and find references for a single ear of grain, a poppy and cornflower . . . and you have all you need for a colourful and evocative fabric painting. The subjects certainly won't be original: but *your* interpretation of them will be.

Cottages, churches, chimneys and children. All can provide interesting shapes which might be simplified to make a textile design. Jot down notes and rough sketches, or take photographs, to remind you.

IDEAS ARE EVERYWHERE YOU LOOK

If the weather is inclement, watch the rain on the window pane; you might paint lines on your fabric, dividing it into squares, then dot abstract blobs of wet colour in each square to suggest the raindrops. Study the simple lines and primary colours of children's toys. Or make the cat sit up so that you can admire the supple lines of its body. Don't attempt a portrait; imagine it silhouetted black against a window so that you sketch only the sleek outline of head, body and curving tail.

Make a cup of tea or a mug of coffee. Teapots and coffee-jugs have inspired many an artist: their homely but interesting shapes can create endless fascinating designs. Of course, there's almost sure to be a pattern or design on the cup and saucer or mug: you might reproduce it to make a matching napkin, place mat or traycloth. Even the spoon might have an interesting shape, or a pattern engraved on it: have you ever noticed?

If you fancy a snack, there's more inspiration in your larder or refrigerator – from fresh herbs to fried eggs! Colourwise, imagine the drama of black coffee swirled with cream; the frosty delicacy of a mixed fruit sorbet; a spicy pizza or a bowl of strawberries. Colour plays such an important part in stimulating the taste buds that the kitchen is a wonderful place to dream up exciting colour schemes: think of the bright green of fresh peas marbled with the clear acid of lemon juice, the rich gold of crusty bread and the wickedly dark chocolate of devil's food cake!

Trace-off designs for the swallows cushion (previous page)

MAKE USE OF EXISTING REFERENCE

Whilst in the library, look for books on subjects which have special relevance. If you're planning nursery curtains for a small boy, a border of small cars in primary colours, bumper-to-bumper, could be fun – or brightly coloured bouncing footballs – or any similar theme which reflects a child's consuming interest. It might be their favourite television cartoon character – or a sporting hero or heroine. Whenever seeking any kind of reference, always turn to children's books first: they often provide the best illustrations – as well as being more basic than those in adult reference books. Remember that concentrating on simplicity of line and shape, with only the barest essentials of detail, will result in the most effective designs.

Obviously books and magazines will provide endless source material. Cut photographs out of magazines when a colour scheme or interior specially attracts you, and mount them in your binder. Study the features on interior design and decor, of course . . . but look at the illustrations to articles on other subjects, too: clothes, gardens, food and travel can all offer up useful ideas.

And don't forget the fashion magazines. You'll find lots of stimulating ideas here: wonderful colour combinations and striking contrasts, especially amongst the holiday and swimwear. Absorb them all and consider how these colourways might be translated into textile designs for your own home.

Visit museums. Study the designs on pottery plates and vases, enamelled items, jewelled decoration, and garments and fabrics from the past. Look at paintings, too. Naturally, ladies and gentlemen wore their best clothes to have their portraits painted, and you will see intricate fabrics from the past accurately copied. You may be able to buy postcards on the way out, reproducing your favourite pieces.

SHOPPING FOR INSPIRATION

When stocking the larder takes precedence over country rambles and visiting museums, you'll find just as much inspiration in your local greengrocery . . . especially in terms of shape and colour. The warmth of sweet, juicy oranges contrasted with the clear, sharp yellow of lemons.

13

Floral design based on an Oriental pattern

(*right*)
The spectacular and instantly
recognisable appeal of batik

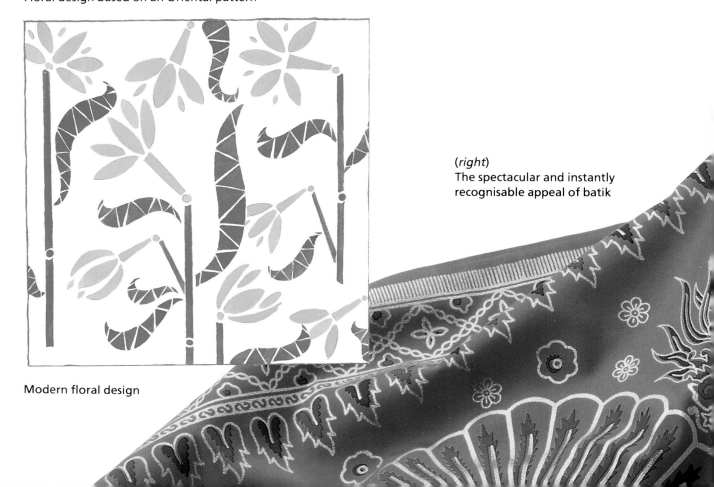

Modern floral design

The widely varied colours of the different apples, from light green to rich burgundy. Notice the subtle difference in colour between strawberries and raspberries. That cabbage which has been cut in half to show its close heart: the incredible way the dark green outer leaves shade inwards to pale cream at the centre. And all the time, compare the shape of everything: from onions, carrots, cucumbers, corn-on-the-cob, mushrooms . . . to the exotic pineapple. Simple shapes like these can be translated into great designs for painting fabric.

Walking around the fabric departments of large stores, you'll be surrounded by ideas. A tiny motif or a colour scheme may set you thinking in another, entirely different direction, to produce a design which appears totally unrelated to the original which inspired it. Incidentally, spare a moment to marvel at the proportion of fabrics inspired by nature!

As your interest grows, you cannot fail to observe how often textile design is influenced by the heavily embossed, painted and decorated cottons, silks and wool from the Oriental and Far Eastern continents. Over the centuries the

designs and patterns have been absorbed into Western decoration – as artists have been inspired by their colour and aesthetic appeal. Perhaps they too compiled source books to inspire them!

It is fascinating to reflect on these original sources, which can be divided into four: Japan, India, Indonesia and China. All closely related, yet each uniquely recognisable in their own right.

JAPAN

The Japanese make everything they do, from cooking to textile painting, an art form. Their constant quest for harmony results in an almost puritanical love of carefully balanced arrangements. Colours are chosen to enhance the particular function of a room, and rice paper screens take the place of dividing walls: Textile design is important in such an environment, both for upholstery and garments, such as the ceremonial kimonos. The latter were superb

examples of highly artistic silk painting, using effective resist barriers, which stop the paint from spreading to other parts of the outlined design (see Gutta: Chapter 10). Exquisite designs would depict traditional legends and symbols representing Japanese philosophy.

INDIA

The mystical legends and religious festivals of India, the jewel-like colours and theatrical culture, are all embodied in thousands of different patterns and textile designs across this vast continent. What Indian fabrics may sometimes lack in quality is compensated by their uninhibited use of different shades, tints and jewel colours, all intermixed to create one dazzling explosion of perfectly co-ordinated design.

The photograph shows an Indian textile painting, circa 1850–1900.

INDONESIA

The people of Java and Bali have developed the

'Batik' wax resist technique (see Chapter 11) in such a way that it has become so much a part of their culture that it is now specifically indentified with these islands. Spectacular designs representing their many religious and cultural festivals have made it one of the largest export materials in the world, and instantly recognisable.

CHINA

For many thousands of years the Chinese have excelled at exquisite flora and fauna paintings on the superb silk fabric which they produce with equal skill. Admired throughout the world, the Chinese style of design infiltrated Western society and eventually became so strong an influence that by the eighteenth century 'Chinoiserie', as it was called, was evident in everything from decor to ceramics. Whilst many ladies of fashion sent lengths of fabric, or pre-cut pieces of garments, to China to be painted and embroidered before being made up.

The photograph shows lychees painted on gossamer organza: water dyes were used for the delicate brushwork (circa 1900).

(*left*)
Chinese lychees on gossamer organza

(*right*)
Indian textile painting, circa 1850–1900

CHAPTER 2

UNDERSTANDING COLOUR AND DESIGN

Like everything else in art – but perhaps *more* than anything else – colour is a very personal thing. Different colours mean different things to different people. But when we talk about something 'bringing colour into our lives', it becomes a metaphor for anything which is entertaining, enjoyable or stimulating, which will cheer us up, relieve monotony, make a break in routine, enliven the daily grind, or give us a fresh outlook. So whatever colour means to *you* – it plays a pretty important part in all our lives!

However one sees colour, it quite definitely influences our senses, emotions, moods – and general feeling of either being 'up' or 'down'. Psychological tests have proved that the colours in our immediate environment can have a profound effect on how we work, feel and behave. Used in the home, colour can create any kind of atmosphere you like. It can make a quiet statement, or an exuberant one: it will reflect light, exude warmth, and generally make a room come to life.

Some people revel in bright, bold colours: whereas others enjoy softer tints and are drawn towards muted, more sedate shades and tones. Whatever your own personal preference, there is plenty of room for diversity. All you need to remember is that the overall effect needs to be balanced and pleasing to the eye, neither overbearingly loud nor depressingly gloomy.

This chapter is all about getting to know colour from the beginning: where the infinite range of colours, shades, tints and tones come from, and how to mix and use them for your painting. At the end of the book we will be thinking about colour again: in the context of planning colour schemes to provide a perfect home for your painting.

When you are planning a project using one of the painting techniques explained in the following pages, you may find it worth turning to the section on Colour in the Home (Chapter 16) in order to decide the colours which will ensure your project looks as if it has been designed specifically to fit the room for which it is intended. Or, of course, if you are planning to paint the textiles for a room which is to be freshly decorated, it is even more important to think ahead to ensure perfect harmony with the colours which will form their environment.

FROM PRIMARIES TO SUBTLE SHADING

The two wheels on this page show how just three basic colours flower into an infinite range of other colours, shades, tints and tones. We begin with these three PRIMARY COLOURS:

Red : Blue : Yellow

The word 'prime' means that they cannot be mixed from any other colour: they are unique. You can see them forming the three large 'petals' which radiate from the centre in Figure 1. Between the pure red, blue and yellow petals you can see what happens when you mix one primary in equal quantities with another. These are known as SECONDARY COLOURS:

Yellow + red = orange
Blue + yellow = green
Red + blue = purple

Finally, the outer petals show the effect of mixing primary and secondary colours. (These are called 'tertiary colours': 'shades'.)

Each colour has a special contrasting colour (known as its 'complementary colour'): this is the

Fig 1 The colour wheel, showing the three primary colours, the secondary colours and the tertiary colours

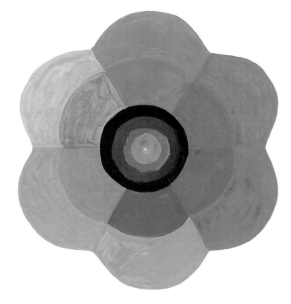

Fig 2 Producing tints and tones

shades of orange that are combined in a sunset – contrasted with the dark blue night sky closing in above.

Figure 2 demonstrates how tints and tones are produced by the introduction of WHITE and BLACK: the flower centre shows them both mixed together to make grey. The shade of grey will, of course, depend on the proportions: begin with plenty of white and a touch of black for a very pale grey . . . and each time you add a little more black, it will get darker.

The original pure colours of all the petals in Figure 2 are exactly the same as Figure 1, but this time they have been muted by mixing with white, black, or a mixture of both. The result shows just a few of the endless range of subtle shades which can be produced in this way, from soft pastel tints, graduating through deeper ones to really dark and sombre tones. (If you make a pure colour lighter, it is called a 'tint', and when you make it darker, it is a 'tone'.)

THE MAGIC OF COLOUR MIXING

The two colour wheels illustrate the theory of colour development very clearly. But mixing palettes is so fascinating: why not have some fun trying out a few simple experiments! Water colours or poster paints will do, if you haven't any proper fabric paints. All you need is the basic pigment palette – in other words, the three primary colours: yellow, blue and red *plus* the basic white and black which will create the subtle tints and tones.

First try mixing the primary colours to make secondary colours:

> **Yellow + red = orange**
> **Blue + yellow = green**
> **Red + blue = purple**

Already you have a wonderful range of possibilities. In addition to the basic primaries, you have an endless variety of secondary colours at the tip of your brush, because *these* depend on the ratio of paint you use. Equal quantities will produce a definite orange, green or purple (as already seen in Figure 1). But the outer petals show what happens when you use more of one primary and less of the other. Try using plenty of yellow and only a little red: you'll have something much cooler – the refreshing colour of chilled

colour on the opposite side of the spectrum. If you study the petals on Figure 1, you will see that yellow contrasts with purple, red with green, and blue with orange. You will find it very useful to remember these complementary colours when you want to pick out an important detail in a design, or add an exciting touch of spice to liven up a colour scheme. A fresh combination of sharp greens, for instance, looks wonderful with a flash of red (think of a woodpecker!). Or imagine all the

When you have mixed some colours you like – try putting them together. Combining two or three striking colours can produce exciting results: the amusing 'Hat Tricks' are smart examples!

Most decorating and D-I-Y shops supply paint shade cards, as well as brochures illustrating suggested fashionable colour combinations. Make full use of these when planning your textile painting. Cut them up and play with the separate squares of colour, rearranging them over and over again, until you find the perfect combination of shades to create the effect you want to achieve. Then, using your newly acquired skills, you will know how to mix the colours you want.

PRESERVE YOUR COLOUR-MIX SECRETS

It is well worth keeping a detailed record of the colours you mix – and how you arrived at them.

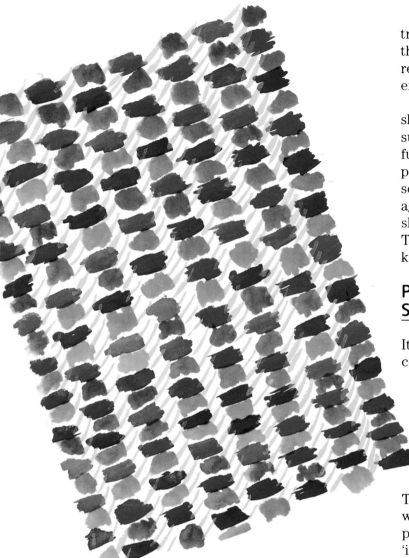

When you have mixed some colours you like, try putting them together

orange juice. Now reverse the mix, using less yellow and more red: the result will be a deep, burning colour like the outer peel of a blood orange or a fiery sunset. By varying your quantities of blue and yellow you can choose the turquoise blue of the ocean – or the fresh lime-green of leaves bursting out into spring sunshine. Purples can be the inviting colour of a glass of Beaujolais – or dark and mysterious.

Finally, when intermixed with white, black, or a combination of both, your pure primaries, secondaries and tertiary shades become tints and tones. You can reproduce whatever you like, from fresh spring sunshine to something warm, sultry and much more intense ... depending on your mood.

Then you will have a permanent source guide which will save a lot of time when planning future projects. This is especially rewarding when you 'invent' a wonderful shade – which is, nevertheless, not what you want for the job in hand. Recorded in this way, you will know how to re-create your discovery when you have found a home for it.

Have a special section in your source book for this purpose (or keep a small separate notebook, if you prefer). Paint the colour on one side of the page, and the mix description on the other side: the colours used, with the exact amount of each, measured in drops (using a pipette) or ml volume.

If you are preparing paints to be used on a large background, try to work out approximately how much you will need to cover the whole piece, and make up a sufficient amount to complete the whole job. It is extremely difficult to re-create *exactly* the same colour, even when the paints are carefully measured. (See Weights and Measures chart: Workshop Section.)

Hat tricks: exploring the use of two
or three striking colours

CHAPTER 3

MATERIALS AND BASIC EQUIPMENT

Once you have started to think about the designs you might paint, and have a knowledge of colour-mixing, you will be impatient to equip yourself for the actual process of painting.

You will need to know the most suitable fabrics to use, the kind of paints to choose, the various methods by which the paint can be applied – and all the incidental accessories necessary to complete your equipment.

As far as the fabrics and paints are concerned, it is all too easy to become confused when faced with the wide variety of fabrics, and their conflicting properties: and in the same way, you can be blinded by science if you try to compare the range of paints and their relationship to the fabrics.

For that reason this chapter gives only a brief outline of the basic facts that you need to know about fabric and paint in general. You will pick up all the practical knowledge as you continue through the book, because the projects and examples that describe each painting technique also advise on the best fabrics and paints to use. Then, when you are ready to plan your own textiles, you will find a 'Workshop' reference section at the end, giving detailed information and advice on each subject. This will enable you to compare the possibilities, before deciding the fabric best suited to the purpose for which you require it – together with the correct paints for that fabric and the technique you plan to use, plus how to apply and fix them.

The rest of this chapter is all about the other items you will need – which are equally important if you want your painting to be easy and enjoyable, as well as successful.

FABRICS

Natural fibres are best – silk, cotton, linen and wool. They absorb paint better, giving the colours brightness, clarity and depth. Designs painted on silk can be particularly spectacular. If using cotton, wash it first to pre-shrink it and remove any special finishes which will prevent it absorbing the paint efficiently. Wool is so absorbent that you will need to double the amount of paint you use: nun's veiling is a good choice, if painting on wool.

Man-made, or synthetic fibre, fabrics are cheaper, and often look and feel very similar to the originals that they resemble: but they are less absorbent, and the results vary considerably. However, you may have difficulty finding 100% pure cotton fabrics, as the addition of man-made fibres makes them cheaper and easier to care for: if this happens, look for a polycotton, or similar blend, with as little additional man-made fibre as possible.

PAINTS

It is important to use the right paint for each particular technique, so check carefully in the appropriate chapter. Unless specifically stated, most paints can be used on the majority of fabrics, but always read the manufacturer's instructions before you begin work.

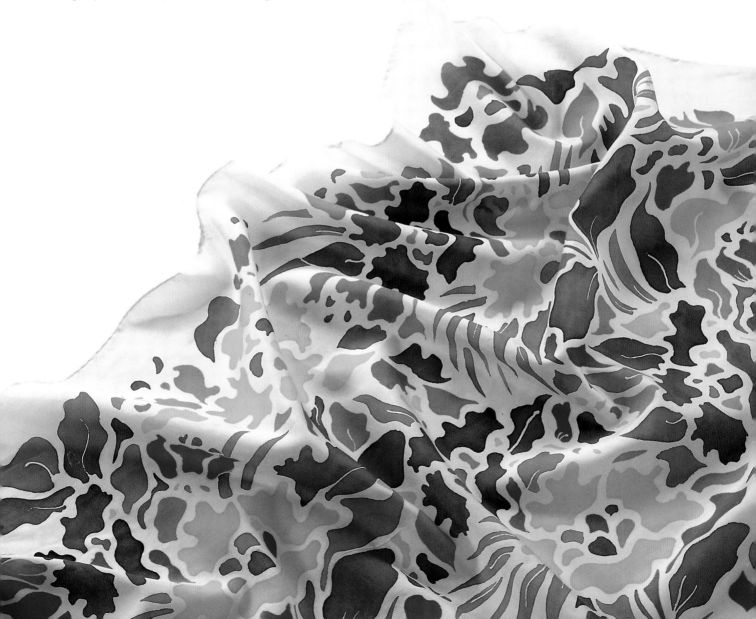

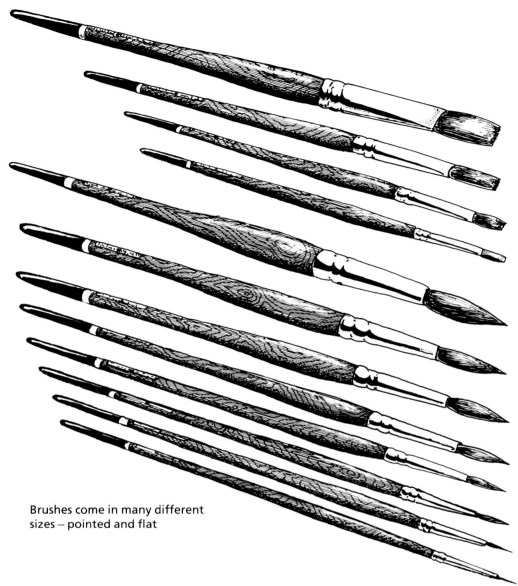

Brushes come in many different
sizes – pointed and flat

Protect your work-table or working surfaces with a wipe-clean cloth or sheets of paper before you begin painting. As soon as you have finished, replace the lids on your jars of paint and put them in a cool place out of direct sunlight.

Never attempt to move your work while it is even slightly damp: leave the fabric on the frame or work-surface until the paint (or gutta/serti) is completely dry. A hand-held hair dryer can be used to speed drying, but don't use direct sunlight for this purpose, as it will affect the colours before they are fixed.

Apart from the actual paints, you can also buy sets of felt-tip pens and wax crayons specially for use on fabric. They are both quick and easy to use, as well as inexpensive, which makes them ideal for children's projects. Both are fixed by ironing, and are fade resistant and fully washable.

These felt-tips and wax crayons are also an excellent introduction to fabric painting, as you can use them for a few experimental projects if you want to try your hand in order to get the 'feel' of the craft. In fact Chapter 5 (Small Beginnings) uses them for this very purpose, showing some simple but colourful examples that demonstrate how versatile and useful these pens and crayons are.

APPLICATION

It is vital to use the correct applicator for the technique with which you are working. These can range from brushes, sponges and cotton wool buds to strange tools from Indonesia! Once again,

24

read the appropriate chapter carefully to ensure you are properly equipped.

One general reminder, which applies to every tool with which you apply your paint, is to clean it immediately after use. Brushes which have been used for water soluble paint should be washed very thoroughly in warm (not hot) water, using a mild detergent. Rinse thoroughly in clear water, then squeeze and stroke them back into shape before leaving to dry, point uppermost, in an empty pot or old mug. Never leave your brushes standing in water. Use turpentine or white spirit to clean brushes used for oil paint. Check the manufacturer's directions on the paints themselves, or accompanying leaflets, to see whether there are any special instructions for cleaning your equipment.

FIXING

There are various methods of fixing to make your painting permanent and washable. Most of the paints used in this book are heat-fixed simply by pressing with a steam iron. There are also paints available that can be fixed with a hair dryer. Other methods involve baking in the oven or steaming in a deep pan, but these are less common, and can usually be avoided.

Salt is a natural fixative, and can be used as an additional precaution against fading when painted curtains or upholstery, etc are exposed to direct sunlight. Mix equal quantities of salt and water, paint with the solution, and allow to dry before washing the salt out again.

BASIC EQUIPMENT

SQUARE FRAME: This is essential for several techniques – and very useful for most of the others. Frames are discussed in detail at the end of this chapter. You can buy them ready-made

from an artists' supplier, or you can have one made specially by a carpenter . . . or you can follow the instructions to make one yourself.

TAMBOUR OR HOOP FRAME A round embroidery frame can be used for the same purpose if you are painting small areas (see page 27).

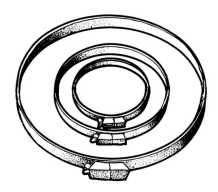

Tambour (or hoop) frames

THREE-PRONGED (ARCHITECTS') PINS Use these special pins to fix your fabric securely when it has to be stretched over a square frame. If you have to substitute an alternative kind of thumb-tack or pin, choose one with a fine, sharp point.

SCISSORS Try to have at least three pairs – and if they aren't instantly recognisable, identify them with coloured tags: one pair for cutting paper; another for fabrics in general; and a super-sharp pair reserved specifically for silk alone.

PALETTES You will need a good supply of these for mixing paints: buy them from artists' suppliers, or use odd saucers, dishes and similar receptacles. Shallow trays in which to stand your paints can be useful if the jars are accidentally knocked over. Wash everything well immediately after painting – it's easier then!

JARS AND POTS OF WATER Two for rinsing brushes: one for light colours, another for dark ones. More for mixing paints, etc.

PLASTIC BOTTLES AND DROPPERS OR PIPETTES These are necessary for certain techniques, and also for measuring paints, as described in Chapter 2.

MARKERS Tailor's chalk pencils are very useful for outlining designs etc on fabric: they can be

Square frame

purchased from needlework/haberdashery shops, and are usually available in white and blue. Maintain a good point with a pencil sharpener or craft knife. The sharp edge of a piece of tailor's chalk may be used for the same purpose: and tailor's chalk in this original form is also needed for the 'prick and pounce' method of transferring designs (see Chapter 4).

The following chapter describes the various methods of marking, and the materials required, in greater detail.

DRAWING EQUIPMENT Pencils, including a very soft (4B) one, a ruler (preferably with a metal edge) and a soft eraser; a sharp Stanley or Olfa craft knife; a black felt-tipped pen can be useful to make an outline bolder before tracing a design.

PAPER Plenty of plain white paper for drawing designs and experimenting with paints, etc (inexpensive sketching blocks and layout pads are quite adequate); tracing paper (ordinary household greaseproof paper will suffice, unless the tracing needs to be more durable for a longer life – in which case, use proper tracing paper); graph paper (for working out designs, enlarging and reducing).

MASKING TAPE Useful for all kinds of purposes: buy a big roll.

PROTECTIVE CLOTHING An apron or overall is always a wise precaution, and it's a good idea to roll up your sleeves when working with paints and dyes. Rubber gloves are necessary for some techniques, like sponging (Chapter 6).

PLASTIC SHEETING Useful to cover your work surface (or you can use *old* newspapers), and occasionally necessary to protect a backing fabric (ie painting a pillowcase – Chapter 7).

SOFT CLOTHS/RAGS AND A ROLL OF PAPER TOWELS Have plenty – for obvious reasons!

WORKING ON A SQUARE FRAME

There are several techniques for which it is essential to have the fabric tautly stretched over a wooden frame. But in many other cases, you will find it makes the painting very much easier, and raising the cloth off the work surface also ensures more successful results.

The frame itself is so simple that it is possible to make it oneself – or else to have one made up by a friendly carpenter. Art and craft shops sell a variety of square or rectangular frames: the more sophisticated versions can be adjusted, either by a slot-in or a sliding system. You can also buy kits, which simply require fixing together with glue or small screws.

MAKING A SQUARE OR RECTANGULAR FRAME

Choose your wood carefully. It needs to be soft, so that you can push the pins in easily: for the same reason, make sure it is not too dry or knotted, and doesn't splinter easily. It is a good idea to ask your timber supplier's advice, explaining what the frame is to be used for, and let him recommend the most suitable wood.

You will require four strips of wood, about 5cm (2in) wide x 12mm (½in) thick: the length depends on the size you want your frame to be. A 50cm (20in) square frame is a useful size for cushions,

handkerchiefs or small scarves, but you may need something bigger, or a rectangular shape, for a larger textile project.

The four pieces of wood must be cut to exactly the same length for a square frame, or two pieces of each required length for a rectangle. The *inside* measurements of the frame will be equal to the actual area of painted fabric, so you will have to add another 5cm (2in) to the length of each side for the border allowance.

MATERIALS

4 pieces of soft whitewood, about 5cm (2in) wide x 12mm (½in) thick, cut to length (see above)

Wood glue, or small nails or staples
Steel rule and set square or T-square
Fine sandpaper
Beeswax

1. Sandpaper the pieces of wood until they are absolutely smooth, to prevent the frame snagging your fabric.
2. Overlap the corners and glue, nail or staple them together, checking to ensure that they are all exactly square: if using glue, leave to dry between clamps – and sandpaper off the excess glue when it has hardened.
3. Rub beeswax very thoroughly into the wood, and your frame is ready for use.

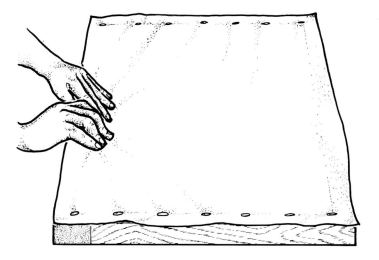
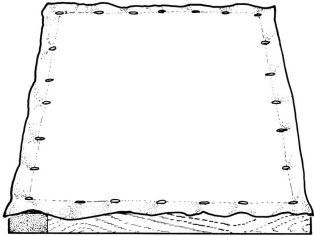

Stretching the fabric onto the square frame

STRETCHING THE FABRIC ONTO THE FRAME

1. Place your fabric underneath the frame and cut it to size, remembering to add a border allowance all round, so that you have a surplus to fasten to the frame: this edge will be damaged by the pin-holes, so you won't be able to use it. (The only way to avoid this happening is to attach the fabric to the frame with masking tape.)

2. (See above). Place the fabric on top of the frame and, holding it steady with one hand, pin it along one side, pushing the pins firmly down through the fabric into the wood. Keep checking to ensure that the fabric remains absolutely straight as you pin: if the grain is allowed to get out of line, the painting will be distorted.

3. Pin the opposite edge of the fabric in exactly the same way.

4. Repeat for the two remaining sides, pulling the fabric gently into place, to achieve a perfectly smooth and even drum-like surface, with a completely straight grain in either direction.

5. Run the palm of your hand over the surface: if the fabric hasn't been stretched correctly, you will feel uneven bumps and sharp edges. In this case, undo three sides and start again.

6. The fabric is now ready for you to start work.

WORKING ON A CIRCULAR FRAME

Tambour embroidery frames provide a useful alternative for small areas of painting. Generally used for needlework, they adapt well for this purpose, and avoid the necessity of pinning or taping the fabric. This type of frame provides a perfectly smooth and even surface to work on, without snags or sharp edges.

The frame consists of an inner and an outer circle: the outer hoop is fitted with a screw/bolt, which tightens it over the inner one when your fabric is in position. (Page 25 shows tambour embroidery frames in three sizes.)

1. Place your fabric over the smaller hoop, and press the outer hoop down on top, so that it fits over the inner one: then tighten the screw.

2. Pull the fabric gently but firmly all the way round, until it is taut and evenly stretched over the frame (see below). Avoid pulling too hard, as over-tightness may damage the fabric.

3. Check to ensure the grain is absolutely straight in both directions.

Working on a round frame

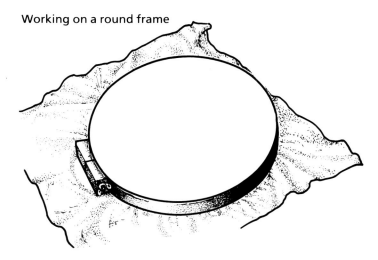

CHAPTER 4

PREPARING THE DESIGN

You are bursting with exciting ideas: you know how to mix wonderful colours: you are fully equipped to start painting. Only two small problems remain: how to prepare the design – and how to get it onto the fabric. When you have found, or made up, a design for painting, the chances are that it won't be the size that you want to reproduce it. There are several ways to make it bigger or smaller, but your most practical method will probably be by using a grid. This is very easy to do – even if you claim you can't draw.

THE GRID SYSTEM

1. Draw or trace your design onto a sheet of paper: if you use tracing or thin layout paper, you can then place a sheet of metric or imperial graph paper behind it, which will help you with the next stage. Pin or tape both sheets securely to one side of your board or working surface.
2. Rule lines around your design, to form a frame: follow the lines on the graph paper beneath to ensure accuracy (use the *bold* lines, so that you have a definite number of centimetres or inches).
3. Now rule horizontal and vertical lines over your design, dividing it into equal squares. These can be any size you wish, depending on the size of the original, but the smaller your squares, the easier it is to make an accurate copy: 2cm (¾in) or 2.5cm (1in) is a good average measure. Make the squares smaller for a complicated or detailed design, but you'll need less squares for something very simple, so you could make them larger.
4. Fix another sheet of paper, with graph paper beneath, alongside the first piece. Rule a frame on this piece, making it *the size you want your design to be*.
5. Rule lines to divide this frame into *the same*

number of equal squares as you have in your first frame (see opposite). For example, if your original squares measured 2cm (¾in) in a 16 x 16cm (6 x 6in) frame, and you want the design twice the size (32 x 32cm [12 x 12in]), your second frame must be ruled into the same number of 4cm (1½in) squares: but if you wanted the design only 'half-up' (24 x 24cm [9 x 9in]), you would rule your second sheet into 3cm (1⅛in) squares.
6. Now, following the squares very carefully, redraw the design over the second grid, making sure that your pencil crosses the ruled lines at exactly the same points on both charts (you can mark these points first, if you like, and then join them up).
7. Exactly the same method is used to reduce a design. Just reverse the process, making your second frame, and the squares within it, smaller than the original.

PHOTOCOPIERS AND PROJECTORS

A photocopier is a sophisticated piece of equipment which can be set to enlarge or reduce a design mechanically in seconds. So if you are fortunate enough to have access to one, take full advantage of it!

A projector can be used to project a design onto a wall or screen, so that you can trace it off. But it is difficult to achieve any degree of accuracy, especially for small designs.

TRANSFERRING DESIGNS
SEE THROUGH METHOD

There are various ways to transfer the outlines of a design ready for painting, depending on the fabric you are using. This is the easiest way, but you can do it only if your fabric is a light colour and fairly sheer.

Place the design underneath the fabric: if it doesn't show through clearly, remove it and intensify the lines by going over them with a black marker. Trace the design onto the fabric with a soft (4B) pencil or other outline marker.

WINDOW METHOD

Use this for slightly darker or denser fabrics. Follow the directions for the See Through Method, but first tape your design to a window, and then fix the fabric smoothly over it. The strong light from behind should enable you to see the design clearly: trace it off in a lighter colour if an ordinary pencil line doesn't show up well.

SPOON RUBBING

Draw or trace your outline onto paper – and check to make sure that the design is reversible. If it *is*, go over the outline with a soft (4B) lead pencil: if it *isn't* reversible, trace it through to the other side of the paper and make your heavy outline on *that* side (you must use a pencil to do this, as other markers won't transfer).

Place the outline face down on your fabric, with a firm surface underneath: then rub smoothly and evenly over the back of the paper, using the rounded blunt edge of a spoon or a coin, or something similar. When you remove the paper, the design should be softly outlined on the fabric; it is usually necessary to draw over it again with a more permanent form of marker.

The grid method for enlarging

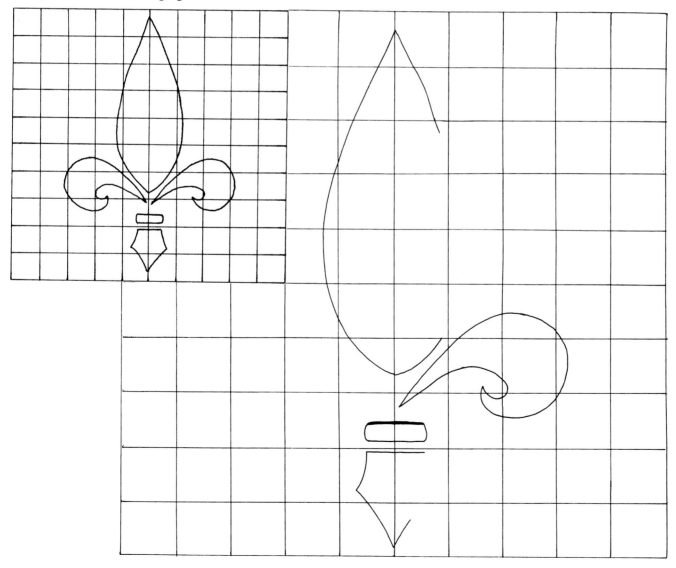

DRESSMAKERS' CARBON PAPER

This can be purchased in several colours, according to whether you are working on a light or dark fabric. Trace your design onto paper in the usual way, then place the sheet of carbon paper face down on your fabric, with the tracing on top. Draw over all the lines with a hard point (a fine knitting needle or similar item), pressing down very firmly. When you remove the tracing and carbon paper, a clear outline should remain: nevertheless, you may need to emphasise this with a tailor's chalk pencil.

LIGHT BOX

This is a more sophisticated version of the window method! It provides a light source behind your work, so that the design can be placed between and seen clearly through the fabric.

A light box can be a great help when working with certain painting methods, especially the gutta-serti technique (Chapter 10), when the fabric needs to be stretched on a frame. The design is drawn or traced onto paper in the usual way. When this is placed on a light box, with the frame over it, the original is seen through the fabric, and the outline can be followed straightaway with the gutta-percha.

The principle of the light box is very simple. Inside a shallow wooden framework (the 'box' need not have a base), two neon strips are attached to the sides, positioned opposite one another. Fixed over the top of the frame, a sheet of glass or perspex forms the 'lid'. When the light is switched on inside the box, it illuminates the top plate, and you are ready for work.

Light boxes can be purchased from most good art supply or graphic shops. Or it is not too difficult to make one yourself. They are a very useful piece of equipment to have in a studio, since they can be used for other forms of artwork too, such as transferring designs and pattern repeats onto surfaces other than fabric, and for viewing slides, etc clearly.

DARK FABRICS

Apart from dressmakers' carbon paper, none of the preceding methods is suitable if you are planning to paint on a very dark background, like black, brown, purple or blue. Nor will an ordinary lead pencil line show up sufficiently. However, there are three ways to overcome the problem.

PRICK AND POUNCE

Draw the design on paper in the usual way. Then, using a darning needle or similar fairly large needle, pierce the paper (pushing the needle well through) every 2mm (1/16in), following the lines of the design very accurately. Go over the whole design in this way.

Crush up a piece of tailor's chalk until it becomes a fine powder.

Place the pricked paper in position on your fabric, then sprinkle the powder over the design and gently brush it in with a blusher or other soft brush.

Remove the paper very carefully, and keep the fabric absolutely flat, in order not to disturb the powdered dots lying on the surface. Draw over these with a tailor's chalk pencil or other suitable marker, joining the dots to form your original design. When you have finished painting, and the work is dry, brush off any remaining chalk.

The pierced paper can, of course, be used over and over again: wipe the underside with a soft cloth before re-using it, to remove any lingering powdered chalk. If you want to repeat a design in reverse, just turn the paper over.

The prick and pounce method for transferring the design onto a dark fabric

CUTTING TEMPLATES

If you are planning a bold design made up of one or more simple, definite shapes, you can make templates of each section and draw round them with tailor's chalk.

Draw or trace (spoon-rub) the design onto quite stiff paper or lightweight card. Cut round the outline of the complete pattern very carefully: then, if it is in several sections, cut along all the dividing lines.

If your design is in one complete piece, place it in position on your fabric and draw very accurately all round the edge, using a white or blue tailor's chalk pencil.

If the pattern is in several sections, place them *all* on the fabric, to ensure that the complete design will appear in the correct position. When you are satisfied, remove the outer sections, leaving only the central one: draw round this as described above, and remove it. Then, one-by-one, place the remaining sections in position alongside the central outline, and draw round them – until the design is complete.

As before, remove any stray chalk with a brush, when the painting is finished and has dried.

TACKING THREAD

This is useful if you want simply to divide your fabric into sections, or indicate the areas of a design before beginning to paint. Just tack along the lines with a running stitch, using a fairly fine sewing thread. Straight lines can often be ruled on with a soft lead pencil, and will be just sufficiently visible for you to follow them with your needle. If this doesn't work, try using a lighter coloured pencil. Simple curves or waves and other geometric forms can be drawn freehand and tacked in the same way. Alternatively, try to visualise the design in your head, and 'sketch' it in with your needle, as if it were a pencil.

Incidentally, instead of removing the tacking when you have finished painting, you might find it interesting to tack with coloured embroidery threads, leaving them in the fabric to create additional contrast, detail and texture.

NOTE: Always use paints that are specially made for dark backgrounds, as other fabric paints will not show up properly.

VANISHING FABRIC MARKER AND TRANSFER PENCILS

The vanishing fabric marker is a special kind of pen which is used to draw a design directly onto the fabric – but the blue or purple ink line later vanishes, either after a few hours, or else in water. You can use a transfer pencil to make your own iron-on transfers. Simply trace or draw your design onto tracing paper (in reverse, if necessary), then iron it onto the fabric.

HALF-ON-HALF

When you want the left hand side of a design to be identical to the right hand side, or the top half the same as the bottom, this method ensures complete accuracy, and saves time.

Fold a sheet of tracing paper in half. Draw or trace one half of your design – positioning it *against the fold* in the paper, so that the fold forms the centre line of the design. Now turn the folded paper over and trace your first outline through onto the other side. Open out the paper and you have your complete design.

Use the spoon rubbing method if you want to transfer the pattern to more durable paper.

This technique can be usefully adapted to make up a design formed from quarters, or when using pattern repeats.

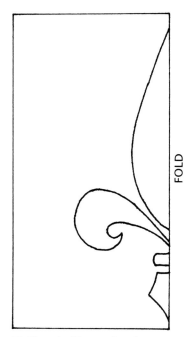

Half-on-half transfer, for a symmetrical design

CHAPTER 5

SMALL BEGINNINGS

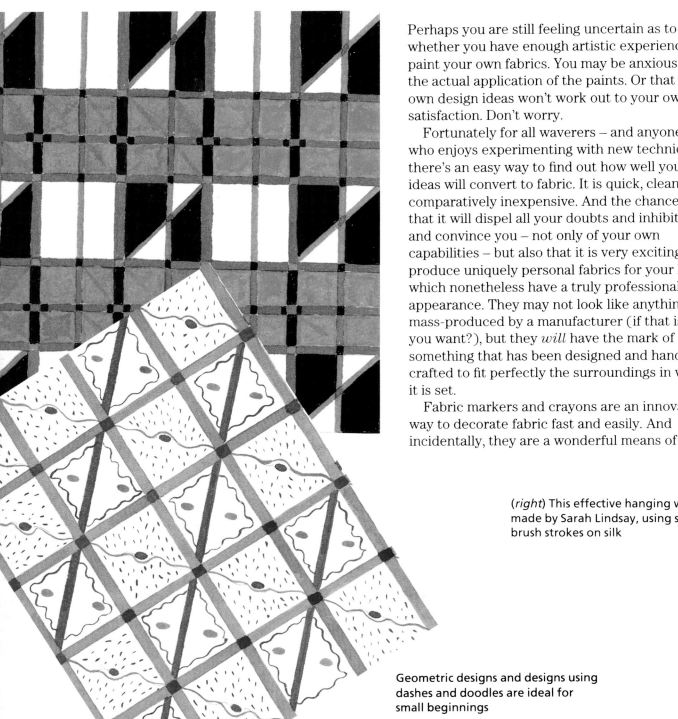

Perhaps you are still feeling uncertain as to whether you have enough artistic experience to paint your own fabrics. You may be anxious about the actual application of the paints. Or that your own design ideas won't work out to your own satisfaction. Don't worry.

Fortunately for all waverers – and anyone else who enjoys experimenting with new techniques – there's an easy way to find out how well your ideas will convert to fabric. It is quick, clean and comparatively inexpensive. And the chances are that it will dispel all your doubts and inhibitions, and convince you – not only of your own capabilities – but also that it is very exciting to produce uniquely personal fabrics for your home, which nonetheless have a truly professional appearance. They may not look like anything mass-produced by a manufacturer (if that is what you want?), but they *will* have the mark of something that has been designed and hand-crafted to fit perfectly the surroundings in which it is set.

Fabric markers and crayons are an innovative way to decorate fabric fast and easily. And incidentally, they are a wonderful means of

(*right*) This effective hanging was made by Sarah Lindsay, using simple brush strokes on silk

Geometric designs and designs using dashes and doodles are ideal for small beginnings

32

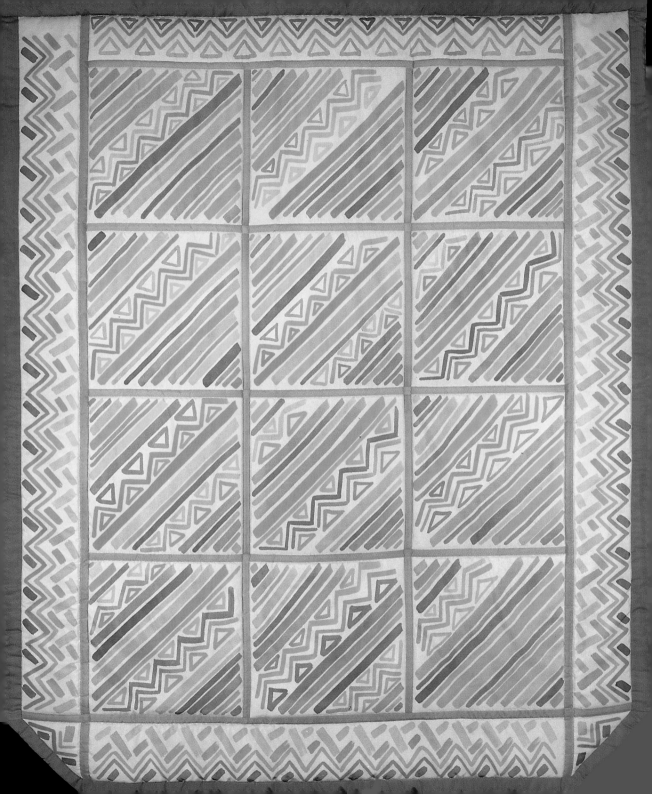

involving even the youngest children in the craft (they are non toxic). If, as we hope, these textile markers persuade you that fabric painting *is* for you, and give you the confidence to explore the many techniques and applications of the craft fully, your introduction to them will not have been wasted. They can often be very effective when used in conjunction with other methods, usually to outline, emphasise or highlight part of a design.

You will find the markers and crayons described fully in the reference section at the end of the book. They are widely available from all art and craft shops, and often from general stationers, too. There are several good makes, and you can buy them in sets or individually. The markers are just like ordinary felt-tipped pens, and are applied in the same way. Some offer a choice of two pens in each colour: one has a fine point for drawing, the other a thick tip for broad outlines and fillings. Other pens taper to a point, so that you can use the tip of the nib for fine lines, and the side for broad ones, shading and filling. Some markers can be refilled when empty, and the worn nibs replaced. Many leave a permanent mark as soon as they touch the fabric, but some allow mistakes to be corrected with soap and water if dealt with quickly while the paint is still wet. Fixing couldn't

be easier: like most of the paints recommended in this book, simply press the fabric on the wrong side for five minutes, using a hot iron.

The crayons are applied in exactly the same way, and are just as easy to use, but take care to place a piece of waste cloth between your iron and the design, to avoid getting wax on the surface of the iron.

Another good method for beginners is a range of paints which, because they are applied a little differently from ordinary textile paints, have the advantage of allowing you to study and assess your design before applying it to the fabric (this is especially useful for children's work). Quite

(*right*)
Paisley shell cushions – an excellent felt-tip marker idea for beginners

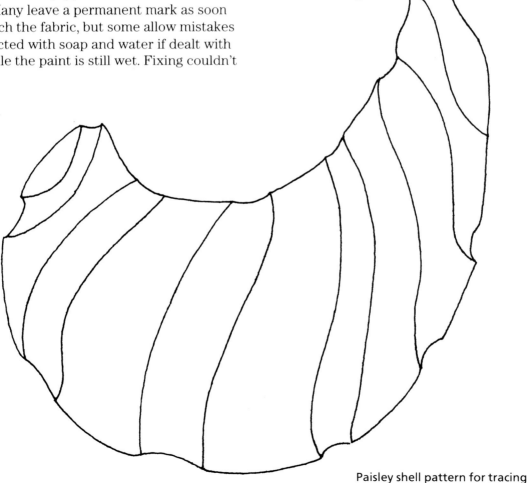

Paisley shell pattern for tracing

simply, the design is painted on a sheet of paper, then transferred to the fabric by ironing over the back with a hot iron. The 'transfer' may be used again, several times, though the intensity of the print will gradually diminish.

All the examples in the illustrations opposite and on page 35 have been worked with the felt-tipped markers, and demonstrate the wide variety of practical and amusing ways in which this technique can be employed. Bleached cotton made a good grounding for all the projects: either sturdy sheeting fabric, or the lighter weight Primissima. Both take the colour very happily, wear well and are easy to sew. Avoid very fine or sheer fabrics, as the colour may spread slightly. Follow the directions in Chapter 4 to transfer or draw out your design, then go over your lines and fill in with the markers, finally iron-fixing as already described.

Paisley variations, geometric designs, or just a profusion of dots, dashes and doodles show how much fun the artist had creating this collection: from the big floppy pillow to tiny scatter cushions for a child-size wicker chair or a doll's bed, and those fat pincushions fixed round your wrist with elastic, that prove so invaluable when you are making up your painted textiles! There are attractive picture frames and a child's shoe bag, too: lampshades, table linen, towels and window-blinds all take well to this versatile form of decoration – even simple dolls and stuffed toys for the nursery.

But perhaps the joy and creative freedom offered by this medium is most eloquently expressed by the charming play rug. A whole class of four-to-five-year-olds combined their talents to put together all their favourite things on squares of unbleached calico, to make their own version of the traditional 'friendship quilt' originally created, and lovingly worked, by the pioneer American settlers.

Felt-tipped markers can be used by complete beginners to make a wide variety of practical and amusing projects

CHAPTER 6

SPECIAL EFFECTS

Your first introduction to working with actual paints is pure fun – yet you are likely to produce some stunning results! Nevertheless, it has a serious purpose, in that it enables you to become familiar with the feel of handling brushes, paint and colour. And it also gives you the opportunity to experience some of the versatile 'tricks' you can play when you introduce sponges and salt to your work.

There are no trace-off designs to prepare: it's simply a matter of painting your fabric freehand – and then letting it all happen! So, to avoid the risk of wasting a lot of fabric, it is best to work out your design first, on a sheet of white paper. This should give you a good indication of the effects which will be created by using various brushes and sponges in different ways, and allows you to experiment with as many colour combinations as

Chesterfield sofa *by Sarah Lloyd*

you wish, before deciding the one which makes the most striking impact.

Children will particularly enjoy expressing their extrovert artistic skills in this way. But the more advanced textile painter can make use of these effects to produce very personal work, as on the chesterfield sofa, where the artist has used different sized brushes to work swirls and circular patterns on the heavyweight cotton fabric.

PREPARING FOR THE EFFECTS METHODS

The spreading and tartan effects are particularly exciting, especially when you use your selection of *brushes* to their fullest advantage: the wider your range of sizes, the more scope you will have for creating diverse and interesting patterns. Experiment on paper to discover their potential:

using the tips of pointed brushes will give you pretty, spotted designs, whereas the straight top of a flat brush dabbed onto the fabric makes short stripes or blocks. Brushes can be used in different directions to create swirls, small lines and tartans.

Virtually any type of suitable *fabric* (Workshop Section) may be used. Just make sure it is right for the project you have in mind, and also for the paints you are using. If it has been treated with any kind of finishing solution in the manufacturing process, wash, dry and iron the fabric before you begin to work on it.

Many types of *paint* are suitable for this kind of work. Silk paints are particularly fluent in application, so run very well into each other when you want a spreading effect, but the heavier type paints may also be used for this technique, and are usually better for the sponge method.

If you are using silk, or another fabric of similar weight and texture, it is best to work on a *frame*. Sturdier fabrics may be laid on a flat surface which is protected by an easy-wipe cover: this is often more convenient for sponging. But it's a wise precaution to raise the fabric if you want the paints to run into one another, as this allows them complete freedom to do so.

SPREADING AND TARTAN EFFECTS
THE TARTAN DESK SET

The pretty desk set in the illustration demonstrates just one attractive way to show this vibrantly colourful method to advantage. The covered board is very easy to make, and the versatile design allows you to adapt it in several ways to suit your own requirements.

Pockets might be added at each side to hold paper, envelopes, letters and notes; the bows decorating the top corners could be replaced with rosettes – or omitted completely, for a more masculine set; flaps could be hinged to each side, folding over to meet at the centre and close the set when not in use; an address book, drum-shaped holder for pens and pencils, and a waste-paper-bin, could all be covered in matching fabric. In the photograph, a strip of left-over tartan has been used to decorate the plain lampshade, but the whole shade might have been covered, in order to integrate it still further into the scheme.

The fabric itself has been painted in the same tartan combination overall: but you could add contrast by having the centre in just one plain colour – or mix plain and tartan fabrics to cover the accessories suggested above.

PREPARING TO PAINT

Use 2-2.5cm (¾-1in) wide flat *brushes* for the tartan effect, reducing or increasing the width of the brush depending how wide you want the tartan stripes to be. A multi-lined tartan can combine several brush widths, ranging from wide to slim, with pointed brushes used to draw fine lines.

Any type of smooth *fabric* may be used, but the desk set illustrated is covered in Antung silk, its natural ivory colour giving a glowing vivacity and warmth to the lilacs and pinks. If the finished size of your backing board is to be approximately 45 x 50cm (18 x 20in), you will need 1.5m (1½yd) of fabric. The width of the silk may differ: try to find one that is at least 90cm (36in) wide.

The *paints* used for this project are Deka-Silk, in pink, violet and azure (medium) blue.

If, as suggested, you are using a silk fabric and silk paints, it is advisable to stretch the fabric on a *frame* (see Chapter 3). However, even if you are using an alternative, a frame is recommended. Not only is it much easier to apply the paints when the fabric is raised, but they will have more freedom to run into one another than if it is laid flat on the work surface, which may also cause smudges and unsightly patches.

When cutting your fabric, remember to add a border allowance to be pinned to the frame.

Use *saucers* or similar receptacles for your paints: don't mix the colours until you are ready to use them. For the project illustrated, the colours have been used straight from the jar without mixing: as you can see, the colours will mix themselves when they meet on the

(right)
The spreading method is used to make the tartan desk set

fabric (see also the tartan pincushion which illustrates the 'salt' technique at the end of this chapter).

Have two *jars of water* for cleaning your brushes, and a *rag* to dry them.

APPLICATION

1. Follow the directions in Chapter 3 to stretch your fabric over the frame, making sure it is smooth and taut, and the weave straight in both directions, when you have finished pinning it.

For other than very fine fabrics, it helps to encourage the paints to spread more freely if you brush the surface with clear water before you begin.

2. Dip your brush into the first colour: if you want to achieve an overall pink tone, start with pink – for a blue base tone, start with blue. Take care not to overload the brush, as this will leave uneven pools on the fabric: always dab off excess paint on a cloth, or wipe your brush on the side of a saucer.

3. Beginning at one top corner of the fabric, draw a vertical stripe from top to bottom: if the stripe loses colour as it reaches the end, repeat the same action – but start from the bottom and work up, to ensure even paint distribution.

Watch the paint to see how far it spreads before you apply the next line: leave a gap of about 2-2.5cm (¾-1in) between each stripe.

Continue to paint vertical stripes in this way right across to the other side of the fabric.

4. Apply the second and third colours in alternate horizontal stripes, working in the same way, but across the fabric from side to side.

Try to work as fast as you can, to allow the wet paints the fullest opportunity to run into one another before they begin to dry: this is the 'effect' you have set out to create.

5. When you have finished painting,

and are happy with the result, leave it undisturbed, and away from direct sunlight, until it is absolutely dry.

When the fabric has been painted in this way, it may be several hours before the paint has stopped spreading and become stabilised in the fibres: so, if possible, wait until the following day before fixing. Leaving it overnight will ensure the paints maximum penetration, which will intensify the colours, and also means that they should have had time to dry: nevertheless, check to make certain that the fabric is absolutely cork dry before fixing.

6. If you have used Deka-Silk paints, press on the wrong side for 3-5 minutes with a steam iron. For other types of paint, follow the manufacturer's instructions for fixing.

Here are some suggestions for alternative tartan effect colour combinations:

SIENNA : ULTRAMARINE : OCHRE
RED : GREEN : YELLOW
PINK : BLUE : YELLOW
PURPLE : RED : GOLD
BLUE : YELLOW
BLACK : WHITE

On the other hand, an equally striking effect may be created simply by painting horizontal lines across your fabric, in an attractive combination of colours and using a variety of brushes to give different widths (see the round pincushion which illustrates the 'salt' technique at the end of this chapter).

MAKING UP THE TARTAN DESK SET

MATERIAL
2 pieces of mounting board cut to the required size (ie 45 x 50cm [18 x 20in])
A piece of baize, felt or gift-wrap paper, same size as the board, to back
30cm (12in) narrow ribbon
Dry-stick adhesive
Clear adhesive

1. Cut the board with a sharp craft knife (see Chapter 3) and a metal-edged rule. Have a chopping board or similar alternative underneath, to protect your work surface. Cut out the inner rectangle: this may be any size you wish – see the diagram for the measurements to make the board as illustrated.

2. Place your fabric right side down on a flat surface: rub the glue stick all over one side of the prepared board, then place it, glued side down, on top of the fabric, leaving an overlap all round. Cut the over-lapping fabric to leave a 5cm (2in) wide surplus all round: then mitre the corners (cut off diagonally, level with the corner of the board, as indicated).

3. Lift up the surplus fabric along one side, turning it smoothly and evenly over the edge of the board, and stick it to the back with clear adhesive. Repeat for the opposite side, then do the other two.

4. Cut away the fabric in the centre, leaving a 2.5cm (1in) overlap. Cut the fabric diagonally at each corner, as indicated. Turn this surplus over and glue to the back of the board as before.

5. Cover the second piece of board in the same way, but don't cut out the inner rectangle.

6. Cut a piece of baize, felt or gift-wrap paper a fraction smaller than your board, and glue it neatly to the back to cover the raw edges of the fabric.

7. To trim with bows, cut two strips of fabric approximately 45 x 12cm (18 x 5in). Fold each in half lengthways and trim off the cut corners at an angle. Allowing 5mm (¼in) seams, stitch the long side edge and both ends, leaving a 5cm (2in) gap at the centre (between notches: see diagram) for turning. Trim the seams neatly and clip the corners, then turn to the right side and slip-stitch the edges of the opening. Tack all round the edge and press. Then knot into a bow.

8. Place the bows over the upper

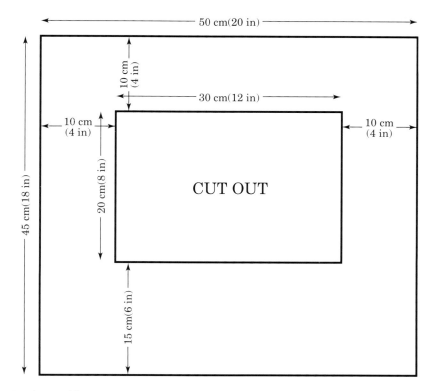

Cutting guide

corners of the top (first) piece of board, moving them around until you are happy with their position. Then make two small holes in the board underneath. Cut the ribbon in half and thread a piece through the back of each bow, then push the ends through the holes in the board and tie tightly together at the back, so that the bows are held firmly in place. Trim off the ends of the ribbon.

9. Glue your first piece of board on top of the second one: if you glue only round the outer edge, you can lift the inner edge of the panel and use the sides as pockets to store stationery, as illustrated.

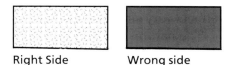

Right Side   Wrong side

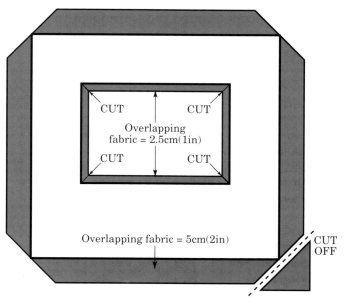

Cut the overlapping fabric to leave a 5cm (2in) surplus all round, then mitre the corners.

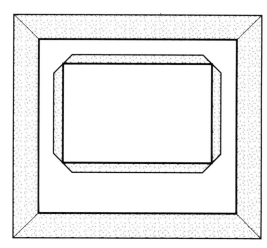

Turn the edges and stick them to the back

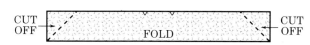

To make bows, fold strips of fabric and trim off the cut corners at an angle

THE PATCHWORK COT QUILT

The result of applying the paint with a sponge is very different from brushwork. It is closer to printing – and somewhat similar to the things that children do with cut potatoes when they first go to school! The sponge effect can be used on its own, to create an interesting textured all-over pattern, or it can be used to form an unobtrusive background for another design to be painted on top. The cot quilt illustrated combines both these effects very successfully.

The natural sea sponge, which comes from the Mediterranean, is the most 'interesting', from a design point of view, because it has large holes in lots of different shapes and sizes. When transferred to your fabric, this natural formation creates a very well defined and fascinating textural pattern.

However, as natural sponges are quite expensive, cheap foam sponges may also be used. Unfortunately the foam is much more dense and even, with only tiny holes, so the closer texture will give a more mottled, all-over effect. On the other hand, this type of sponge may be cut into flowers, leaves, crescents, stars or different geometric shapes, with interesting results. You can even buy amusing bath sponges shaped like hands and feet, for a fun project!

Sponges are also very useful for stencil work – or you can design impressive patterns with the help of masking tape. Layering colours one on top of another creates depth and dimension, and fabrics sponge-painted in this manner can be very effective when used for piping on cushions, curtain tie-backs and applied edgings.

PREPARATION FOR SPONGING

Both natural sea *sponges* and the cheaper foam variety are stocked by most chemists' shops and department stores.

Again, most *fabrics* are suitable for sponging. The important thing is to choose the sponge and paint most suited to the surface texture of the fabric you want to use. For instance, a natural sea sponge is necessary to achieve a visible effect on fine silk, as foam sponges leave only a blurred design after the paint has spread. A natural sponge was used on the cotton cot quilt, to give a fairly distinct effect, but a foam sponge could have been used for a softer design.

The result you want to achieve will dictate the type of *paint* that you need to use. On the whole, the

thick consistency paints are more successful than the thinner ones, which have a tendency to run and spread, especially on silk. The thicker paints work equally well on silk and cotton, and with both kinds of sponge. Deka-Permanent was used for the cot quilt.

If you are planning to work on a border, make stripes or create a pattern of squares or diamonds, you will need a roll of *masking tape*. This forms a barrier which prevents the paint reaching the masked fabric, dividing the sponged areas as you wish.

Use long strips of tape, either horizontally or vertically, to make stripes: keep the strips absolutely straight and even, measuring the distance between them at frequent intervals, to ensure complete accuracy. The diagram shows how to create diamond patterns by

crossing the tape diagonally.

When using two or more colours, allow each colour to dry before applying the next, as it is all too easy to transfer wet paint inadvertently from one masked section to another.

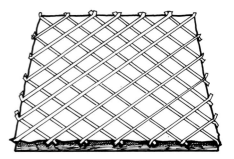

To create a diamond pattern for sponging, use masking tape.

(*right*) The cot quilt uses sponge effects for the background and the all-over pattern

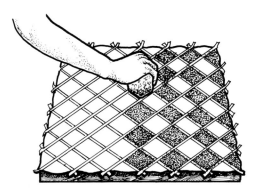

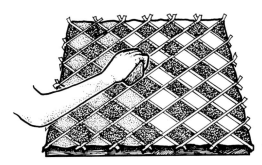

Allow each colour to dry completely before adding the next

You will need *flat saucers*, or something similar, for your paints. And small *bowls of water* to rinse the sponges: have a separate bowl for each colour. Keep a roll of *paper towels* handy on which to dry your sponge after rinsing: if it is too wet when dipped into the paint the result will be blotchy.

Cover your *work surface* with some kind of wipe-clean protection (ie plastic sheeting) before you begin sponging. It's a good idea to protect your hands with *rubber gloves*.

APPLICATION

1. Prepare your fabric as previously described, then spread it flat on the work surface, adding masking tape if required (see above).
2. Prepare your paints on separate saucers.
3. Rinse and dry the sponges (one for each colour).
4. Dip your sponge into one saucer of paint and test the strength of

colour on a spare scrap of fabric. When you are satisfied with the result, press the sponge very lightly onto the fabric: too much pressure will spoil the effect. Continue to dab the sponge lightly over the fabric until the whole area is evenly printed. If you want a more intense colour, you can make a second application when the first layer has dried.
5. When you have finished, leave the fabric until it is completely dry. (It may be hung on a line.)

FIXING

If you are making the cot quilt using the recommended paints, wait until it is finished before fixing (but if you have used a paint that requires steam or solution bath fixing, it must be done before the fabric is made up).

Otherwise, press fabrics painted with Deka-Silk or Deka-Permanent paints on the wrong side for 3-5 minutes, using a steam iron.

Check the manufacturer's instructions for fixing other paints.

MAKING UP THE PATCHWORK COT QUILT

MATERIALS

1.25m (1¼yd) medium-weight white cotton sheeting, 228cm (90in) wide (or an equal amount of a similar alternative)
Deka-Permanent paint: yellow and red
1m (1yd) thick washable wadding
6 large self-cover button mounts
Matching threads

NOTE: In addition to the equipment already discussed, you will need a medium-size pointed brush to decorate the border.

A natural sponge was used for the quilt illustrated.

1. Cut your fabric in half to make two 1.25cm (1¼yd) lengths. Put one aside and cut the other in half

again: sponge one of these pieces with yellow paint, and the other with red.
2. When completely dry, cut each piece into eight 20 x 25cm (8 x 10in) 'squares'.
3. Allowing a 1cm (⅜in) seam allowance, join all the squares to form one piece of patchwork, as shown in the photograph. Open out, trim and clip the seams, and press them flat.
4. Tack the wadding to the back of the patchwork and cut it level with the fabric.
5. Place the remaining fabric right side down on a flat surface. Pin the patchwork, wadding side down, on top: tack together. Cut the backing fabric, leaving a 6cm (2½in) overlap all round.
6. Fold this surplus neatly up over the edge of the patchwork and pin. Turn the raw edge under and slip-stitch neatly all the way round to form a border (trim off excess to avoid bulkiness when folding the fabric over at the corners).
7. Paint the border freehand with a brush, making a zig-zag/spotted design, as illustrated.
8. Cover the buttons with painted fabric, and stitch between the patches or in your preferred position. Stitch right through all the layers of fabric when sewing on the buttons, and draw the thread up tightly, to form the quilted effect. Quilt the other corners of the patches in the same way, making your stitches show as little as possible, and finishing off securely at the back.
9. Press the quilt thoroughly with a steam iron to fix the paints (unless you have already used an alternative process).

SALT ON FABRIC EFFECT

THE PINCUSHIONS

One of the most popular 'tricks' in fabric painting is the sprinkling of salt onto wet fabric. The results are remarkable – and always different. The action of the salt causes the paint to move about and retract, creating fascinating and often dramatic patterns on previously painted fabrics. Sugar causes a similar reaction, but to a much lesser extent. Alcohol also causes the paint to react strangely, and can have exciting results: but salt is by far the most practical method of producing this effect.

The two pincushions in the photograph are made from fabrics which have had the salt treatment after painting with the 'spreading' method – illustrating how two different effects can be combined to produce an even more artistic result. Salt can also be used to great advantage in combination with the Gutta-Serti Technique (Chapter 10), highlighting chosen areas of a design within the resist barriers created by the gutta.

Once you have decided your colour scheme, the most important consideration is to choose the fabric and paints which will encourage the best results.

Two pincushions made from fabrics which have had the salt treatment after painting with the spreading method

PREPARATION FOR THE SALT EFFECT

The most effective results are achieved on *silk fabrics* of fine to medium weight. Lightweight, and finely textured, cottons may also be used, but the effect won't be as dramatic on cotton or woollen fabrics.

It is important to wash, dry and iron fabrics first, in order to remove any special finishes used in their manufacture.

Only *silk paint* is suitable, because the very runny consistency provides the necessary wet surface on which the salt must be sprinkled: it will not react in the same way on thick, dense paints.

Coarse *sea salt* is the ideal choice for really stunning results! Ordinary table salt, which is finely ground, will also produce interesting patterns – but they won't be as dramatic.

It is essential for the fabric to be tautly stretched over a *frame* (Chapter 3). Not only is this necessary when working with wet paints on fine fabrics, but if the fabric is laid flat on the work surface, it inhibits the action of the salt and prevents the paints reacting fully.

Use a *large flat brush*, as speed is important when applying the paint. If you want to add more interest and texture to the design, add a layer of *sponge* work when the salt has dried and been removed.

Use *saucers* or *small dishes* for your paints, if you are not using them straight from the jar. Have *two pots of water* and a *rag* for cleaning brushes.

APPLICATION

1. Stretch the fabric on the frame (Chapter 3).
2. Paint on the colours, moving quickly.
3. Immediately you have finished painting, sprinkle salt onto the wet

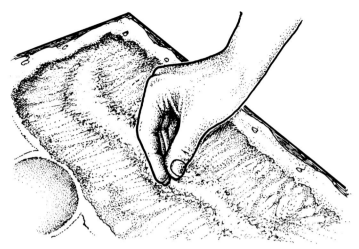

Sprinkle salt on the fabric, wherever you want its effect

surface, wherever you want the effect to take place. It is important to do this quickly, as nothing will happen once the paint has dried.
4. Leave the fabric on the frame, preferably overnight, until it is absolutely dry.

FIXING

Remove the fabric from the frame, brushing off all the salt crystals very thoroughly. If you have used Deka-Silk paints, press on the wrong side for 3-5 minutes, with a steam iron. Fix other paints according to the manufacturer's instructions.

MAKING UP THE PINCUSHIONS

MATERIALS
A piece of painted silk or very fine cotton, about 45cm (18in) square
Plain lightweight cotton to back (see steps 1 and 2)
Polyester stuffing
Matching threads
Ribbons to trim, if required

1. Cut a paper pattern the size and shape you want your pincushion to be. The ones illustrated are 15 x 18cm (6 x 7in) and 17cm (6¾in) in diameter.
2. Decide which is the most attractive area of your fabric, place your pattern over it, and cut it out.

Cut the pattern twice more in plain cotton. If you have any painted fabric left over when you have cut the frill, use it for the back of the pincushion: otherwise use the backing fabric on its own.
3. Measure the four sides, or the outer edge, of your pattern, then cut 5cm (2in) wide strips of painted fabric for the frill, joining them together to make a strip about twice this measurement. If cutting the strips along the straight of the fabric prevents you appreciating all the colours to the full (ie the tartan), cut them diagonally on the cross. Join bias strips on the straight (forming a diagonal seam). Join the ends of the strip to form a circle. Trim the seams and press them open.
4. Place the wrong side of the painted front of the pincushion over the right side of one piece of backing fabric and tack together. (Repeat for the back if using painted fabric: see step 2.)
5. Wrong side inside, fold the frill in half lengthways and tack. Then gather about 5mm (¼in) above the cut edge.
6. Mark the frill into four equal sections with pins: for the rectangle, adjust slightly to make two sections a little longer, with the shorter ones between, to accommodate the different measurements of the sides. Sub-divide each section into

four again.

7. Mark each side of the rectangle into four equal sections. Mark the edge of the circle into four quarters, then mark each into four.

8. Matching the cut edge of the frill to the cut edge of the front of the pincushion, and right sides facing, pin the two pieces together, matching the marked points: then draw up the gathers to fit (the outer, folded, edge of the frill will be towards the centre of the pincushion). Tack together, then stitch along the gathering line.

9. Pin the front and back pieces together, right sides facing and frill inside. Join all round, following the previous stitching line, but leaving about 5-6cm (2-2½in) open at one side, for turning.

10. Trim and clip the seams and corners, then turn to the right side.

11. Stuff fairly firmly, pushing the filling well into the sides, as well as the corners of the rectangle.

12. Turn in the edges of the opening and slip-stitch neatly together.

13. Trim with ribbons, if you wish.

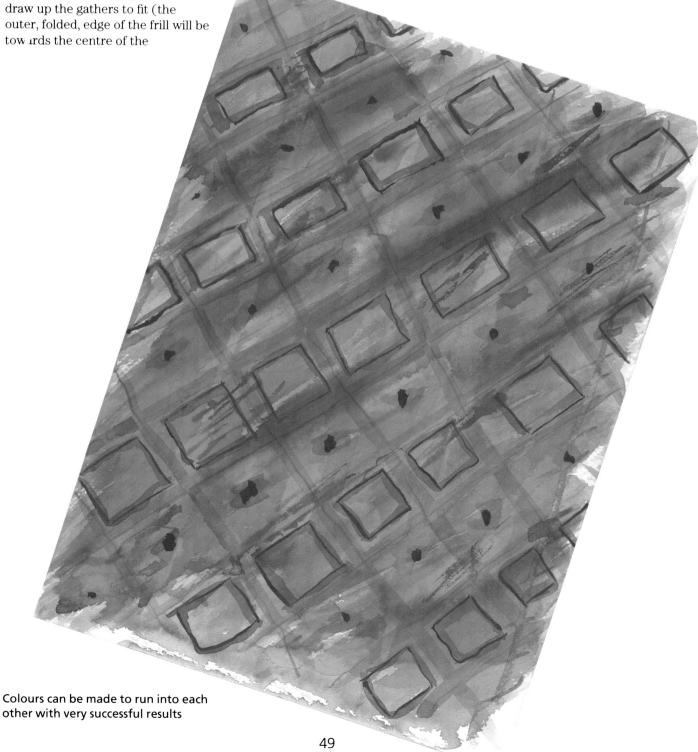

Colours can be made to run into each other with very successful results

CHAPTER 7

DRAWING AND PAINTING

Having experimented with designs which almost create themselves, we now turn to the much more formal technique of drawing out your design on the fabric – and then painting it in. The process itself is very similar to working on paper or canvas. The basic equipment of brushes, pencils, etc remains the same: only the paints will be different.

The design itself has to be your own choice: the scope is limitless. You may have already decided exactly what it is to be, and how you plan to arrange it on your fabric. Perhaps you will turn to your source book for inspiration, and develop a design from the notes you have made. Or you might study the work of other designers, to see the strange and interesting way in which style, taste and fashion changed in the relatively short space of time between the late nineteenth century and the 'thirties, and the influence that the past has had on design today.

If you look at any kind of classical art before that period – whether in painting, sculpture, furniture, ceramics or textiles – you will immediately notice one thing about whatever is represented: it had to be realistic. Flowers, always the most popular subject, had to be as close to the original as the artist could make them. In shape, colour and form they often resemble botanical specimens. No-one ever dared to question Nature's supremacy in the field of design: probably because it never occurred to them to do so.

Designs and patterns to inspire the fabric painter, by Eugene Grasset, Ad & M. P. Verneuil and Karl Leuth

Not, that is, until the turn of the century, when the appearance of what became known as 'Art Nouveau' suddenly changed everything. The origins can be seen earlier than this, in the work of William Morris: whilst retaining their realism, Morris simplified the natural lines of his plants, birds or animals to create beautifully balanced, flowing designs. But the French artist Eugene Grasset was a leading influence in the Art Nouveau movement itself, highly acclaimed for his distinctive floral textile patterns. Although his flowers kept their natural proportions, lines and colours, he gave them a gently abstract treatment, which resulted in a greatly simplified and stylised version of the original. The graceful, smoothly curving lines and subtle, shaded colours of Art Nouveau were an antidote to the heavily cluttered and rigid formality of nineteenth century ornament and decoration. The lightness and freedom of this new art form came as a breath of fresh air to the stifled Victorians.

Although Grasset's work was revolutionary in comparison to previous design, it still adhered to certain basic aesthetic rules. But once Art Nouveau had caught the public's imagination, others sought still further change, and from this emerged an even greater simplicity of line in the much more dramatic and extremely colourful 'Art Deco'. This far more radical development was not so easily accepted, until some of the most highly regarded traditional designers turned to it with enthusiasm. Then this even more modern art quickly gained popularity amongst the fashionable younger generation, its excitement and bold abandon perfectly matching their energetic and fun-loving lifestyle.

And then it seems as though time suddenly stood still. Because if you look at textile design today, you will recognise all three styles firmly in evidence. Your favourite department store offers a choice of furnishing fabrics which depict nature in its more realistic form, including many William Morris classics, which are still as fresh and popular as ever – alongside designs which were clearly inspired by the graceful, flowing curves of Art Nouveau or the simple shapes and vibrant exuberance of Art Deco.

Perhaps this understanding of contrasting forms of interpretation of the same subject will give you food for thought as you turn the pages of your source book. That rosebud which looked so beautiful on a summer morning; the wrought iron gate which caught your eye; the strangely fascinating shape of a pineapple . . . All have tremendous potential for development – in several completely different styles.

TO DRAW AND PAINT

Choose the thicker type of fabric *paints* for this kind of brushwork: these are almost poster-paint like in consistency, which prevents them being absorbed into the fibre of the cloth as the more fluid silk paints, or dyes, would be. This is most important in order to preserve a clear outline and keep the paint within the design you have drawn. Once the paint penetrates the fibres of the fabric, your outline will become blurred.

Your *fabric* needs to be firm, closely woven and have a fair amount of 'body'. Lightweight and sheer silk fabrics are not suitable, because they are too fragile to take the weight of the thicker type paint described above. Medium-weight cottons are ideal, as they have just the right amount of resistance: so if you are planning another type of fabric, bear this in mind as a comparative guide.

As usual, wash, dry and iron the fabric to remove any manufacturer's finish.

A clear outline of the design to guide your

This striking tablecloth could be worked using several of the techniques described in this book – either individually, or combining one method with another. Stencils, gutta and batik might all be employed, but drawing and painting would be equally suitable, following the procedure described in this chapter. Simply enlarge the flower design from the diagrams overleaf, using the grid system explained in Chapter 4. Use a firm, smooth cotton, but choose your paints to suit your mood. The vividly colourful version illustrated conjures up exotic alfresco meals served on a shady patio to escape the sultry heat of midsummer. But delicate pastels and soft tints – perhaps matched to the design on your favourite tea set – would suggest a gentle, more formal, occasion

brush is essential, so find the *marker* which works best on the particular fabric you are using (see Chapter 4). On light fabrics a soft pencil, a water soluble marker, or a self-fade pen are the most efficient methods.

Have a B, 2B or 3B lead *pencil,* or a light coloured pencil if you prefer – and use a craft knife or sharpener frequently to retain a very sharp point. Keep the lines of your drawing fairly faint, whilst making sure the whole design shows up clearly. The pencil marks should not be visible when you have painted over them, even with light colours, and will eventually wash out.

Water soluble markers are ideal for this kind of work. After fixing the paints, the line will disappear as soon as it comes into contact with water.

Self-fade markers are equally suitable. Paint inside the blue or purple outline – and it will begin to fade gradually after a few hours (it may take two or three days to disappear altogether).

(*above*) Central design and (*right*) corner design for the floral tablecloth (page 53). Enlarge using grid system

On darker fabrics, use a well-sharpened *tailor's chalk pencil* to draw the design – grinding a *piece of tailor's chalk* into a fine powder if you are using the 'prick and pounce' method first.

On the other hand, for a bolder effect, an *outliner* will add another dimension – either to the whole design, or to selected areas. *Felt-tip pens* are excellent for this purpose: black and coloured outlines will give the painted sections within much greater importance. *Gutta* outliners (see Chapter 10) may also be used for additional interest: the coloured ones have a metallic sheen, which can be used to great effect (experiment with a small brush to spread the outline: you may find it enhances your design still further).

The size of your *brushes* will be determined by

the size of the design. Small, pointed brushes are necessary for delicate detail, but increase the size of the brush to cover larger areas.

Drawn and painted designs can often be even more attractive when combined with another technique. For instance, a *sponge* could create a gently mottled background (see Chapter 6). Or your design could be painted over a backing of soft stripes, sponged with the aid of a roll of *masking tape* (also Chapter 6).

Traced designs can cause problems because of the necessity to use a heavier weight fabric. Even if it is a light colour, you may not be able to use the see-through method without the assistance of a *light-box* or *window* (Chapter 4).

You will need the usual *palettes, saucers* or *small dishes* for mixing colours, *jars of clean water,* absorbent paper towels and/or *soft rags.*

Cover your work-surface with a *protective sheet.* And it can be a good idea to wear an *apron* or *overall.*

APPLICATION

As has already been pointed out, there is little difference between painting on fabric and painting on paper or canvas. If you are proficient

in the latter, you will understand the importance of building up layers of colour to create shading and achieve the required effect. If you are inexperienced, it is worth experimenting first on paper, using poster paints. Begin with the basic colours: then see how your design gains shape and form with subtle shading, using white and black to create tints and tones for light and depth (as explained in Chapter 2). Any craft book giving advice on the technique of painting will be useful if you feel you need further guidance.

1. Trace or draw the design onto your fabric as already discussed.
2. Pour out the paints and mix your colours.
3. Paint the design as described above. If you wish to paint over previously painted areas, wait until the first layer of paint is dry: otherwise the second colour will mix into the original one, and defeat the effect that you are aiming to achieve.
4. When you have finished, leave the work undisturbed to dry, preferably overnight.

FIXING

Follow the manufacturer's instructions to fix the paints, making sure they are absolutely dry before you begin.

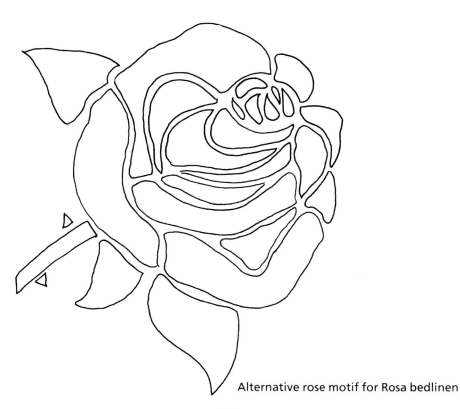

Alternative rose motif for Rosa bedlinen

THE ROSA BED-LINEN

Create a romantic dream by decorating plain white bed-linen with a delicate rose design picked out in soft, dusty pastels (see overleaf). Add a patchwork quilt and lacy drapes to complete the nostalgic mood. This feminine design adapts beautifully to decorate lampshades, cushions, curtains, duvet covers, quilts or headboards.

In this case your *fabric* will consist of two normal size white pillowcases, and a single (or double) sheet.

For the design as illustrated, you will need Deka-Permanent *paint* in white, red, azure (blue), medium green and brown (or you can mix blue and yellow to make green, and then add red to make brown). (Use special Deka-Deck paints if you are working on a very dark background.)

Assorted *brushes* should range from fine to medium, and have good points.

You will need some *plastic sheeting,* either the same size, or slightly smaller, than the pillowcases.

Markers and *painting equipment* as already described. You will also need an ordinary *black felt-tipped pen* with which to trace the design.

APPLICATION

1. Trace the rose and bud separately, using the felt-tipped pen to make a heavy black line on your tracing paper.
2. Spread out the top of the sheet, folding it over as it would be in use (ideally, do this on the bed itself). Then lay your tracings on top, moving them around to decide where and how to arrange them to create an attractive pattern. You could alternate the rose and bud along the edge to make a formal border; have a border of roses and scatter the buds across the sheet above; or make a random pattern of both all over the sheet.

Mark the centre point on both tracings, then use your marker, or pins, to indicate where that point falls on the sheet every time the

Rosa bedlinen motifs for tracing

design is repeated. (Begin at the centre of the sheet and work across to each side, using a ruler to ensure an equal distance between the motifs.)

3. Place one of the tracings on your protected work-surface with the top of the sheet over it, position so that the appropriate design falls as you want it, centre points matching. Trace the outline carefully. If you cannot see it clearly enough, use a window or light box (Chapter 4).

4. When you have finished transferring the traced roses onto the sheet, plan out the design on the two pillowcases in the same way. Place a piece of plastic sheeting inside each pillowcase before tracing the design, and leave it there to protect the back of the pillow until you have finished painting, and the paint is dry. Remove the plastic before fixing.

5. Mix your paints to create pastel shades for the flower petals. Begin with a white base and slowly add red until you have just the shade of pink you want: in a separate saucer, add blue to some of this pink to make violet. In the same way, prepare your green and brown for the leaves and stems, adding white to soften them into pastel tints. If you want a very natural green for the foliage, mix in a little brown.

6. Carefully paint the petals and leaves, beginning with a layer of light colour, then adding darker shades to give shape and form (study the photograph for guidance).

7. When you have finished painting, leave everything undisturbed until it is absolutely dry.

FIXING

For the paints described (Deka-Permanent) press the fabric on the wrong side for five minutes. For other types of paint, follow the manufacturer's instructions.

(*right*) The Rosa bed-linen

THE 'PETALS' LAMPSHADE

A plain lampshade takes on a completely new personality after a brush with some fabric paints! This pretty design of colourful petals on a lilac ground has a decorative edge touched with gold.

Choose a paper-backed cotton-type fabric *lampshade*.

For the colour-scheme illustrated, use Deka-Permanent, or similar *paints*, in black, white, cerise, yellow and blue.

You will also need a *gold gutta outliner* (see Chapter 10 for full details) and a selection of fine to medium *brushes* with good points.

Fix the shade to a *lamp base* when you paint it: this will not only hold it steady, but make it much easier to work on.

A *marker* to outline the petals on the shade, and *painting equipment,* as already described. If you are tracing the petals design, use a *black felt-tipped pen* to make a heavy outline on the tracing paper.

APPLICATION

1. Either trace the petal designs from this page, or else sketch your own versions on a sheet of paper and, when you are satisfied with the shapes, trace those. Alternatively, draw the petals freehand directly onto the shade.
2. Draw petals all over the shade, using the most suitable fabric marker for the purpose: either transfer your traced design (see Chapter 4), or else draw them freehand, as suggested above.
3. Fix the shade on the base, ready for painting.

4. Prepare your paints. Mix white with cerise to make dark pink: mix blue and yellow for green, then add white to give a soft pastel tint. Use black and yellow on their own.
5. Paint in the petal shapes with these four colours, following the illustration for guidance.
6. When the paint is dry, draw round the petal edges with the gold gutta outliner. Then fill in the background between the petals with a series of evenly spaced spots.
7. The top edge of the lampshade in the photograph has been painted black, then dotted with spots of gold. The bottom edge is also decorated with gold spots, this time

interspersed with a small green stripe made with the tip of the brush.

FIXING

It is not necessary to fix the paint on the lampshade, as this will be done automatically by the heat of the lamp.

The plain lilac napkin which covers the table on which the lamp stands, is painted in exactly the same way: fix according to the manufacturer's instructions.

(*right*) The 'Petals' lampshade

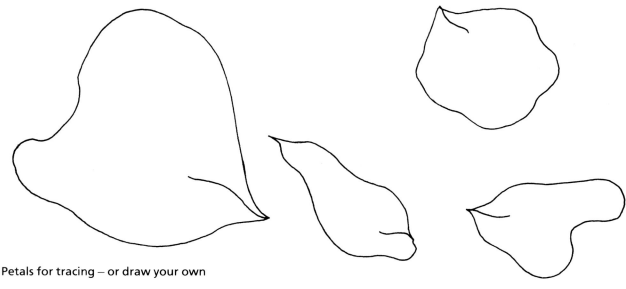

Petals for tracing – or draw your own

ROLLERBLINDS

Rollerblinds, whether used alone, as an alternative to curtains, or in conjunction with them, are extremely useful. They also provide a wonderful painting ground – making the window the focal point of a room. If the blind is framed by curtains, these could be the same colour, and painted with a matching design – or the same design might be repeated in different colours.

Be sure to measure your window frame very accurately before purchasing your blind. You may have to order it specially, but if your window is a standard size, you should be able to buy one ready-made. Rollerblinds also come in D-I-Y kit form.

The *fabric* is treated with a special stiffening solution, which allows the blind to be repeatedly unrolled and pulled up without losing its smooth appearance. Never wash rollerblind fabric, as it will remove this stiffening solution.

Deka-Silk paints or similar types of *silk paint*

are ideal for this purpose. In the case of rollerblinds, there is no danger of the paint spreading, because the solution with which the fabric has been treated will prevent this happening.

Bright primary colours create especially striking results, but those used for the Kimono blind are secondary colours: Deka-Silk paints in azure blue, pink and black, with a gold gutta outliner providing the detail decorating the front neckline of the kimono.

(Note: if you wish to fix the paints afterwards, choose a type which is heat-fixed by ironing or a hair dryer.)

Use large flat *brushes* to paint in large areas, and smaller, pointed ones to do the detail work.

You will need *small dishes* for your paints, together with a suitable *marker* (soft pencil or alternative), and the other *painting equipment* already discussed.

APPLICATION

1. Unroll the blind on a large work-surface or a clean floor area.
2. Using a soft coloured pencil, transfer your design, or draw it freehand, making sure it will be positioned correctly when the blind is hanging at the window. If you are copying the Kimono blind, measure and draw the lines with a ruler: either make up your own kimono, or base your design on the pattern for the wallhanging in Chapter 10.
3. Place the teapot design (see overleaf) underneath the blind and trace it onto the canvas as illustrated.
4. Paint the teapots, using a medium pointed brush, and working from the outside towards the centre.
5. Paint in the background area with a large, flat brush, but use a smaller brush around the teapots. Start at the top and paint downwards, working as quickly as possible to prevent streaking.
6. Leave to dry: if you use a hair

dryer, hold it at least 20cm (8in) from the canvas. Don't roll up the blind until it is absolutely dry.

FIXING

If using the recommended paints, press on the wrong side with a hot iron for five minutes. For other paints, follow the manufacturer's instructions to *iron-fix only*. Otherwise, do not fix.

(*right*) The kimono rollerblind

Teapot motif for rollerblind

Alternative rollerblind design

(*right*) TURKISH DELIGHT
A thousand and one nights of mystery are encapsulated in this magical setting! A subtle feeling of masculinity is conveyed by the strong colours and bold geometric patterns: deep cream and beige plus plenty of

cosy cushioning add the softening touches that give this window seat its theatrical air, resplendent with luxurious comfort.

Bold purple and beige stripes are very effective on the festoon curtain, whilst the rollerblind has an unusual scallop-cut bottom edge, finished with a narrow purple border to set off the cream design. The same understated wash pattern is repeated on the fabric used to upholster the oblong cushions lining the window seat itself, but again

there is a touch of purple in the piping around the edge.

The round scatter cushions are painted in beige and burnt orange, with the shape of the gothic design followed for the scalloped edge. Behind them carpet bag cushions in purple and deep plum, with thick cord piping and ornamental tassels, add an exotic finishing touch.

Use medium-to-heavy-weight cottons for the drapes and upholstery, and masking tape (see Chapter 6) to ensure that you paint perfect stripes every time. The curtain may be draped permanently, if you wish, with the rollerblind drawn to cover the window when required

Design for Turkish delight cushion

CHAPTER 8

DECORATIVE BORDERS

Painted borders are a wonderful way to introduce an element of decoration to a plain fabric without losing its overall neutrality. They can transform curtains, bed-linen, bath towels, cushions, tablecloths, placemats and napkins: and they are equally at home on walls and furniture, especially when a stencil is employed to repeat the design (Stencilling: Chapter 9).

The two floral patterns illustrated on pp 70-1, 74-5 make a striking comparison. The first design is a delicate combination of pastel tints, and would work equally well merging into a soft pastel background or standing out against the contrast of a dark one. The clearly defined flowers in the second example are dominant in themselves, but their bright colours are even more striking seen against a dramatic black background. Both designs are strips which can be repeated to make a border as long as you wish.

Do try some border designs of your own. They are very easy, and great fun. Work your ideas out on strips of paper, remembering that one end must match up with the other, so that they can be repeated over and over again. Begin with simple shapes like triangles, squares and circles set between straight and broken lines. When you have

mastered the technique, try building up more intricate designs with leaves and flowers (it's perfectly legitimate to add a few squiggles to fill in the awkward bits!). Once you have accomplished this type of design, you should be able to attempt any kind of border with confidence.

When you come to transfer the design to the fabric, measure the length of the 'block' – and also the finished length you want your border to be. The finished border must be a multiple of the single block, so you may want to plan carefully where the border begins and ends, to achieve a balanced effect. Graph paper will help.

Most of the techniques described in this book can be used to make borders. Apart from straightforward drawing and painting (Chapter 7), stencils (Chapter 9) are ideal because they make the repetition so easy: resist barriers (Chapter 10) make it possible to use lightweight fabrics; felt-tipped markers, wax crayons or iron-on fabric paints (Chapter 5) are excellent for quick and cheerful results; and the special effects methods (Chapter 6) lend themselves perfectly, either creating a background for another technique, or to make colourful edgings and bindings to cheer up plain fabrics.

(*right*) GARDEN ROOM
A beautifully co-ordinated combination of soft, mellow colours and floral patterns contrives to bring the peaceful terraced garden into this light and airy room. The warmth of rosewood and mahogany doorframes, curtain fittings, floorboards and occasional tables helps to emphasise this subtle effect of a room at one with nature.

The curtain borders (see pattern on page 72) may either be painted straight onto the fabric, or else worked on separate strips of the same or contrast fabric, and applied to the curtains afterwards by machine or hand sewing.

The lampshade repeats the floral design, this time without the border. A plain wooden painted base picks up the restful green of the leaves.

The tulip detail which edges the border design has been enlarged to make a stencil to partner the drawn and painted pattern. Using special stencil paints (see Chapter 9), the tulips have been worked on a ground to match the curtains, then the strips appliquéed onto a soft grey rug. The stencil could also be used to make up a frieze for the walls, or to stencil furniture

Border design *by Paul Sparling:*
pattern on page 72

Pattern for tracing, from the design
on pages 70-1

Pattern for tracing, from the design
on pages 74-5

Border design *by Paul Sparling:*
pattern on page 73

CHAPTER 9

THE ART OF STENCILLING

Stencils offer a whole new field of applied design. Identical repetition, as many times as you wish, is perhaps their most obvious facility. But they have many other advantages and attractive facets, too. The craft of stencilling has been practised for many thousands of years: but now, with modern materials and paints, this simple but fascinating technique promises even more exciting exploitation for fabric painters.

Appropriately, it was the Chinese, inventors and pioneers in paper-crafts, who turned their expertise to cutting shapes out of paper to make templates for painted designs. Layers of paper were pasted together to form a firm board which was soaked in linseed and other oils. When the board was dry, the design would be cut out.

Sometimes bold angular shapes were stencilled on to form the basis of a design: then the fine detail would be painted in with a brush afterwards. Alternatively, an intricate stencil might be built up by the use of several sheets of different cut-outs, working one layer of pattern over another until the design was a complete whole.

Stencilling reached Western Europe in the mid sixteenth century, where it soon became so popular that European settlers naturally introduced it when they built their new homes in North America. Wallpaper was only a luxury for the rich, but even if it had been available to everyone, it wouldn't have been practical on uneven plastered walls, which bulged and sloped in all directions. Stencils provided the perfect

STENCIL KIT
Foreground: stencil brush; drawing pencil; cutting knife
Left to right: rag; sponge; car spray-paint; Deka Permanent paint (350ml bottle); mounting spray; linseed board; plastic stencil sheet

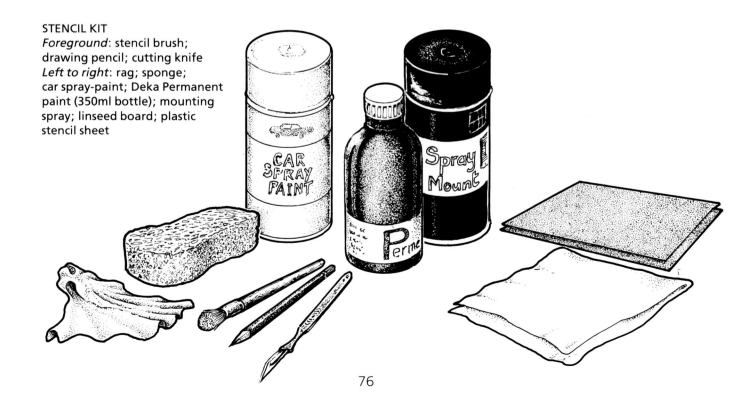

DUTCH COLONIAL DINING ROOM *by Adele Bishop* (USA). A variety of different stencils were used to bring light and colour into this formal dining room. At the same time demonstrating several very effective uses for border designs, as discussed in the previous chapter.

Blue and red flowers edge the filmy white cotton muslin drapes at the sash windows, softening any tendency to hard lines and square angles of the room itself. At each side of the windows a stencilled urn carries an abundance of climbing roses which echo the red in the curtain design, whilst the blue is repeated in an elegant frieze which runs round the room below the ceiling. Both colours reappear in a delicate border stencilled above the painted panelling covering the lower part of the walls

Cream placemats are perfect against the warm glow of a polished mahogany table: the stencilled borders harmonise with the deep blue and green painted ground, patterned with flowers, of the Colonial style chairs

answer, and 'interior decorators' travelled the countryside with their collection of patterns. Many were traditional and symbolic designs, and the stencil artists performed their art on whitewashed walls, repeating the motifs on wooden furniture, and sometimes textiles, too. Fascinating examples of their craft have been preserved in the early American settlers' homes, and can also be seen decorating quilts, often combined with another handicraft, such as patchwork.

Present-day domestic paint manufacturers seem to offer new varieties, in an even wider range of colours, every year. And paint now plays such an important part in interior decor that designers experiment enthusiastically with different forms of application and interesting painting techniques. So it is not surprising that stencilling has enjoyed such a popular revival in recent years.

Ready-designed stencils and special paints are available in an abundant choice of designs, suitable for every room in the house, though their bold but simple shapes, and potential for the use of bright colours, make them specially attractive for children's rooms. Little ones enjoy repetition, too: Carolyn Warrender's nursery (illustrated in Chapter 16) is a charming example.

Modern pre-cut stencils are made from more durable materials like rigid plastic, so that they are virtually indestructible. These are quick and easy to use, since they need no preparation other than pressing out the shapes. But there is a great deal of enjoyment and satisfaction in cutting the stencils yourself. It also means that you can create original designs, specifically to suit your own decor and express your own personality.

Stencils can also be used to advantage with other forms of painting: providing a background effect, superimposed on another design, or forming a basic shape for further decoration.

THE STENCILLING TECHNIQUE

Stencil material is stocked by most good art and craft shops. It comes in two forms: either the traditional linseed-soaked stencil paper, or special plastic sheeting, known as stencil film. The transparent stencil film is very helpful when matching up, if you are using several stencils for one design.

A very sharp, fairly flexible *knife* is essential, with plenty of spare blades. A Stanley knife is good for heavy work: but the Olfa knife, which has a long blade composed of a series of snap-off sections, or a surgical scalpel, are the most suitable for more delicate or detailed cutting.

Always cut against a *ruler* when you want a straight line – and make sure it has a metal edge.

Also very important is your *cutting board*. This should have a perfectly smooth and even, very hard surface: a wooden board is the best substitute for a special *cutting mat,* which you can buy from artists' suppliers.

First work out your design on paper, then transfer it to the stencil sheet (see Chapter 4). Experiment with very simple shapes to begin with, like squares, triangles, circles or semi-circles. Place the stencil sheet on your cutting board and

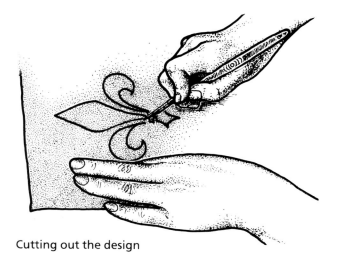

Cutting out the design

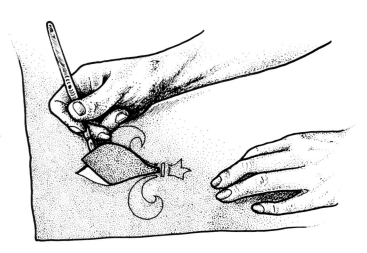

Lifting out the cutaway section

use the point of your knife to cut the shape out, pressing down firmly and working slowly and carefully, to ensure an absolutely clean cut edge. Hold the knife só that it rests between your thumb and forefinger, with the index finger over the top. Keep the blade as straight as possible, to ensure a smooth, clean edge. Apply pressure at the head of the knife with your index finger, but don't press too hard, or you will impede the smooth, fluent movement of the blade: take special care around circles and curves.

Lift out the cutaway shape with the point of your knife, cutting any small areas which fail to dislodge. This is important, because if you push the pieces through from the back, any un-cut areas will leave torn and jagged edges.

Having cut out the shape or shapes (make sure you leave an adequate border all round to keep the stencil rigid and firm), you could add strips of

Applying paint to the flat end of the stencil brush

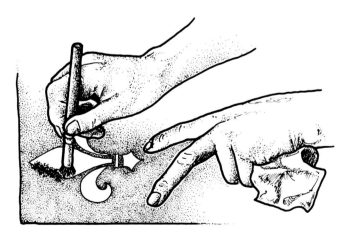

Dabbing paint onto the fabric, working from the outer edge inward

masking tape across the cut-out area, about 1.5-2.5cm (½-1in) apart, to form stripes or a diamond pattern.

As you become familiar with handling the knife, and your skill increases, you will soon realise the potential for this kind of design, and want to progress to more delicate stencils. Remember that if you want to make more than one colour application, or your design has a lot of intricate detail, you will need to cut several stencils, so that you can apply the paint in phases.

PREPARATION FOR STENCILLING

The traditional stencilling *fabric* is calico or bleached cotton. Although almost any fabric *may* be used, some lend themselves considerably better than others. Those most closely resembling a firmly woven, medium-to-heavyweight cotton are the most suitable. However, if you are particularly anxious to stencil onto finer fabrics, such as silk, wool or fine cottons, it is possible to do so (see below).

It is important to use a very dense *paint*, in order to prevent it seeping under the edge of the stencil and blurring the outline. Deka Permanent, or any other paint of a similar consistency, should prove satisfactory. There are some paints on the market which have been specifically developed to eliminate the danger of smudging when stencilling on textiles, and these are often referred to as 'stencil paints'. Nevertheless, take special care when you apply any kind of paint, in order to avoid under-edge leakage and retain a sharp, clearly defined outline.

As already explained, *silk paints* are very fluid, which makes them unsuitable for stencilling because the thin consistency would lead to under-edge leakage. Nevertheless, a special thickener may be used which makes the paint into a paste, suitable for stencilling on silk, wool and fine cotton: this will prevent smudging when applied with a stencil brush to fine fabrics.

There are some *alternative paints* with which you might like to experiment. Most garages and D-I-Y stores sell spray cans of *car paint*. This is useful for some forms of stencilling: but for textiles, only heavyweight cottons are suitable. It can be heat fixed by ironing. Do take great care if using these sprays, and work in a very well ventilated area, as the fumes can be dangerous.

Two excellent mediums, clean, easy and ideal for children, are *felt-tip fabric markers* and *fabric crayons.* They fill in the design with bold colour, without any danger of smudging, and the shape can then be further embellished with additional freehand decoration, using markers or crayons in other colours.

Stencil brushes are quite different from ordinary paint brushes. The round brush is a dense mass of short bristles which, instead of diminishing towards a pointed tip, are cut straight across to form a flat stubbled surface with which the paint is dabbed on, all over the cut-out area (see diagrams on page 79: applying paint to the brush, and applying the brush to the fabric). Choose the size most suited to your stencil.

Another method of application is with a *sponge* (see Chapter 6). Interesting effects can be achieved, depending on the type of sponge used.

You will need *saucers* or *small dishes* for your paints (a very shallow dish if you are sponging); *jars of clean water* to wash your brush, and absorbent *paper towels* or a *soft rag* with which to dry it; a roll of *masking tape*; *newspaper* or a *plastic sheet* to cover your work-surface.

APPLICATION

1. Wash, dry and iron the fabric to remove any manufacturer's finish.

2. Prepare your stencil as already described.
3. Prepare your brush or brushes, or other applicator, and set out the paints.
4. Lay your fabric out on the covered work-surface: if necessary, fasten it down with tape to hold it in place.
5. Place the stencil in position and fix the corners with tape to prevent it moving.
6. Pour some paint into a saucer or dish, mixing the colour if necessary.
7. Dip your brush or sponge into the paint and then dab it on a paper towel or some spare fabric to remove any excess. Apply the paint as already described, using a brush or sponge, and working from the outside towards the centre, to avoid a build-up of paint around the edge. Leave for a few minutes.
8. Carefully remove the stencil from the fabric and wipe any paint off the back with a paper towel or rag, if you intend to use it again. If you are building up a design with several stencils, leave each layer of paint until it is completely dry before applying the next one.
9. When the paint is quite dry, remove the fabric from the table for fixing.

FIXING

Follow the manufacturer's instructions for the paints you have used.

THE FLEUR-DE-LYS BREAKFAST SET

The timeless elegance and simple shape of the fleur-de-lys motif makes it a perfect subject for stencilling this smart breakfast set. A sponge is used to give the feathery effect.

To make the set as illustrated, you will need *four quilted placemats* in blue (or an alternative dark colour) and *two table napkins* in cream.

If, as illustrated, you are working on a dark fabric, use Deka-Deck special *dark background paint*: in this case the colour is yellow. Use normal paints for a light background: in this case, Deka-Permanent in dark blue.

A *natural sea sponge* was used to create the light, very open-textured effect.

You will also need the *stencil making materials* already discussed (tracing paper, stencil sheet, cutting mat/board, sharp knife, etc); a *shallow dish* into which you can dip your sponge easily; *jars of clean water,* absorbent *paper towels* and/or a *soft rag; newspaper* or a *plastic sheet* to cover your work-surface. As usual, protect your clothes with an *apron* or *overall,* and roll up your sleeves.

(*right*) The fleur-de-lys breakfast set

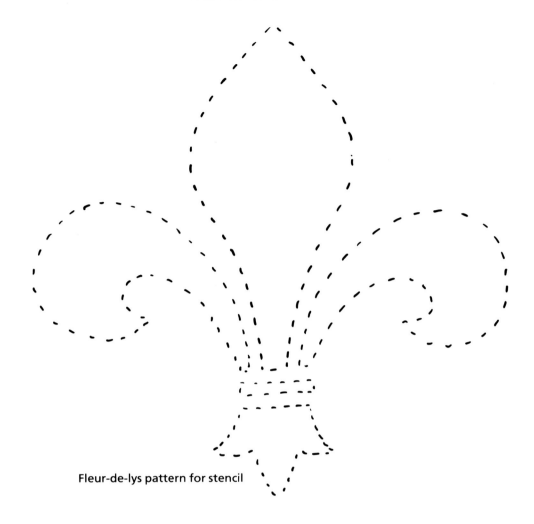

Fleur-de-lys pattern for stencil

APPLICATION

1. Trace the fleur-de-lys outline onto your stencil sheet, and cut it out very carefully, as already described.
2. Lay the stencil (or the tracing) on a placemat to determine where and how you are going to place the motifs: mark the position of each motif. Mark identical positions on a second placemat. Then, on the two remaining mats, work out the arrangement of the motifs for the teacosy, following the photograph for guidance.
3. Position the stencil over one marked point on a placemat and tape the corners to prevent it moving.
4. Pour some paint into the dish and dip a dry sponge into it. Dab it onto

a spare piece of fabric or paper towel to check it is not overloaded, then sponge over your stencil design, using a light dabbing movement.
5. Wait a few minutes, then very carefully lift off the stencil and wipe the back to remove any paint. Place it in the next position and repeat for the other two motifs. Stencil the second placemat, and the two for the teacosy, in the same way.
6. Stencil a dark blue fleur-de-lys in each corner of the two napkins.
7. Leave everything until it is thoroughly dry.

FIXING

If using the recommended paints, heat fix by ironing on the wrong side for five minutes. For other

types of paint, follow the manufacturer's instructions.

TO MAKE THE TEACOSY

MATERIALS
Two painted placemats as above
Matching thread

1. Mark the top corners of each teacosy placemat with a pin or thread, then pin them together, right sides facing and corners matching.
2. Mark a curve across each top corner.
3. Tack the mats together, then sew, by machine or hand, following the marked lines and leaving the lower edges open.
4. Trim off the corners, then turn inside out and press out the seams.

'TEDDY BEAR' TOY-BAG AND DECKCHAIR

A very different, but equally popular, subject with all ages. The Teddy Bear gives you the opportunity to build up a design with three layers of colour, using a separate stencil for each. Transparent stencil film is better than oiled board when you have several stencils, as it makes it so much easier to match them up exactly. Deckchair canvas, and the sturdy unbleached calico used for the toy-bag, are both ideal for stencilling, and this amusing design works perfectly on them – providing you with relaxation in the garden, and encouraging Junior to tidy up!

PREPARING TO STENCIL THE TOY-BAG

To make a bag of a similar size to the one illustrated, you will need 2m (2yd) *unbleached calico*, 90cm (36in) wide (it may be narrower, if you prefer, but not less than 60cm [24in]). Machine along the cut edges with a zig-zag stitch to prevent fraying.

Deka-Permanent *stencil paints* were used, in black, white, red and cerise.

A medium *stencil brush* is best for this stencil: the background is filled in with small, flat brush strokes.

Stencil making materials, masking tape, painting equipment and *protective coverings*, etc, as already discussed.

APPLICATION

1. Fold the fabric in half widthways, right side outside. With the fold at the bottom, mark (with pins or faintly with pencil or chalk) a line 10cm (4in) from the top (cut) edge (this will be the channel for the draw-string). Also mark a faint line at each side 2.5cm (1in) from the selvedge, for your seam allowance.

Teddy Bear stencil patterns (third part overleaf)

2. Trace the bear, then lay your tracing on the fabric to decide how you are going to arrange the repeats for the design (don't go too close to the side seams or top channel). Measure the distance between the repeats very accurately, and mark the position of each bear carefully.

3. Trace the design in three parts to make your three separate stencils, each time tracing *only the broken lines,* so that you cut out those sections only. When you have done this, letter each stencil as shown.

4. Place stencil A in the first position at the top of your fabric, and fix the corners in place with masking tape.

5. Pour some white paint into a saucer and add red to make pink: then add a little cerise to make a slightly darker shade.

6. Dip your brush into the paint, then dab it on a paper towel or rag to remove any excess: stencil the fabric as already described. Immediately remove the stencil very carefully and wipe the back to clean off any stray paint.

7. Repeat steps 4 and 6 for each bear. When all are done, leave until quite dry.

8. Tape stencil B over the first partially painted bear, exactly matching the position. Stencil the fabric as before, using pink paint (mix cerise and white).

9. Repeat for each bear, then leave until dry.

10. Tape stencil C into position over each bear, to stencil the black areas. Add a touch of darker colour to the inner ear, for contrast.

11. Fill in the background with short red brush strokes, as illustrated.

12. When the paint is absolutely dry, turn the fabric over and repeat on the other side of the bag.

FIXING

If using the recommended paints, press the back of the fabric for five minutes with a hot iron. For other paints, follow the manufacturer's instructions.

MAKING UP THE TOY-BAG

MATERIALS
Prepared fabric as above
2m (2yd) cotton or satin rope or thick piping cord
Matching thread
Large safety pin

1. Right side inside, pin and then stitch the side seams, ending 10cm (4in) from the top edge: reinforce the top 3cm (1in) by stitching over the seam three or four times.

2. At each side, and on both sides of the bag, turn back the remainder of the selvedge above the seam to form a hem, and stitch.

3. Fold the top 5cm (2in) over to the wrong side and stitch to form a channel for the draw-string rope.

4. Turn the bag to the right side.

5. Bind each end of the rope or cord very tightly with thread, about ten times, to prevent it unravelling, finishing off very securely.

6. Fix the safety pin through one end of the rope or cord, then thread it through both channels. Remove the pin and knot the ends tightly together.

PAINTING THE TEDDY BEAR DECKCHAIR

Special *deckchair canvas* is stocked by many department stores, or may be obtained from specialist suppliers. Measure the length required for your chair, remembering to allow extra for fixing to the rail at each end. Alternatively, buy a ready-made deckchair with plain canvas.

The *paints* and *other equipment* are all as described for the toy-bag.

Having decided and marked the proposed positions of the bears, follow the directions for stencilling and fixing the toy-bag. *But* use pink paint for stencil A, black paint for stencil B, and red paint for stencil C.

(*right*) The 'Teddy Bear' toy-bag and deckchair

C

THE 'FAIRGROUND ATTRACTION' DECKCHAIR

A charming design, reminiscent of beautifully painted Victorian roundabouts.

You can see this lively design again in Chapter 16, decorating a chest in the delightful nursery stencilled by Carolyn Warrender.

Measure and obtain your *deckchair canvas* as described for the Teddy Bear project.

On the deckchair shown, the blue and red horses have been quite softly stencilled with *felt-tip fabric markers*. Then the red and blue decoration has been worked on top with Deka Permanent *paints,* for a much bolder effect.

Apply the paints with a small *stencil brush.*

The same paints were used for the stripes, which are sponged on between strips of *masking tape,* using a natural or foam *sponge.*

You will find it much easier to match up the design if you use *transparent stencil film.*

You will also need all the other *stencil making materials* previously described, and the usual *painting equipment* and *protective coverings,* etc.

APPLICATION

1. Trace the two horses, then lay your tracings on the canvas to decide how you are going to arrange the design, at the same time fixing masking tape in place for the stripes (remember to leave surplus fabric at top and bottom for fixing to the rails). Measure the position of each horse accurately and mark the canvas where each design is to fall.
2. Trace the design for each horse in three parts to make three separate stencils, each time tracing *only the broken lines, so that you cut out those sections only. When you have done this, letter and number each stencil as shown.*
3. Place stencil A1 in the first position at the top of your fabric, and fix the corners in place with masking tape.
4. Stencil the horse with a red felt-tip marker, smudging the colour to give the body a very subtle, soft effect. To do this, draw a thick line on the edge of the *stencil* (not the fabric); then, while the paint is still wet, use your fingertip to smudge it over the edge and onto the fabric. Work all the way round the edge of the horse in this way until the whole animal is depicted in a spread of gentle colour. Stencil the pole with a blue felt-tip, using it normally, to make a strong line.

When you have finished, remove the stencil and wipe it clean. Then tape stencil B1 into position beside your first motif, and stencil it in exactly the same way.
5. Repeat stencil A1 below the first motif, but this time stencil it with the blue felt-tip, smudging it as before. Stencil a bold red line for the pole.

Repeat stencil B1 alongside it.
6. Continue to stencil pairs of horses in alternate colours, to the bottom of your canvas. Leave until dry.
7. Tape stencil A2 over your first horse, matching the position exactly.
8. Pour out some blue paint. Dip your brush into the dish, then dab it on absorbent paper or a rag to remove any excess. Stencil the fabric as already described. After a few minutes, remove the stencil very carefully and wipe both sides to remove any stray paint.

Tape stencil B2 over your second horse, and stencil the trappings in the same way.
9. Use stencils A2 and B2 to decorate all the remaining *red* horses with blue paint. Leave until quite dry.
10. Repeat steps 7, 8 and 9, using stencils A2 and B2, but this time decorate all the *blue* horses with *red* paint. Leave until dry.
11. Tape stencil A3 over your first horse and repeat step 8, but use *red* paint to stencil the mane, saddle and remaining decoration. Repeat with stencil B3 for your second horse. Continue until you have done all the *red* horses. Leave to dry.
12. Repeat step 11 for the *blue* horses, using *blue* paint. Leave to dry.
13. Sponge the stripes with red paint (see Chapter 6). When dry, remove the masking tape.

FIXING

If using the recommended paints, press the back of the fabric with a steam iron, following the manufacturer's instructions. For other paints, follow the manufacturer's instructions.

(*right*) The Fairground Attraction deckchair (*design courtesy of Caroline Warrender*)

A1

Stencil patterns for 'Fairground Attraction' deckchair

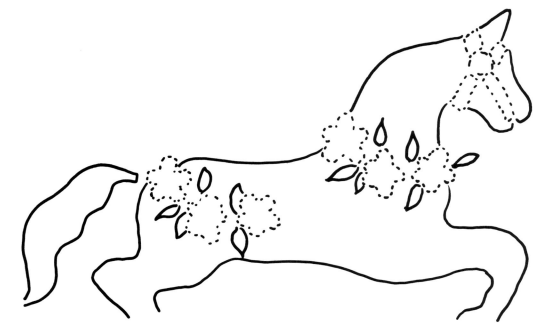

A2

B1

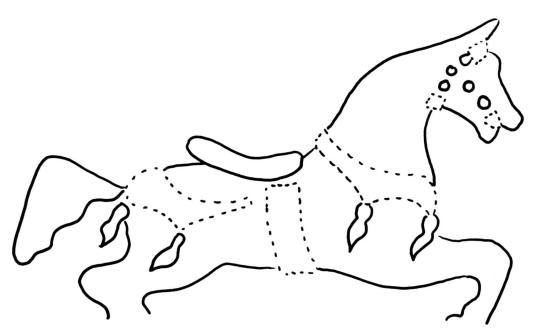

B2

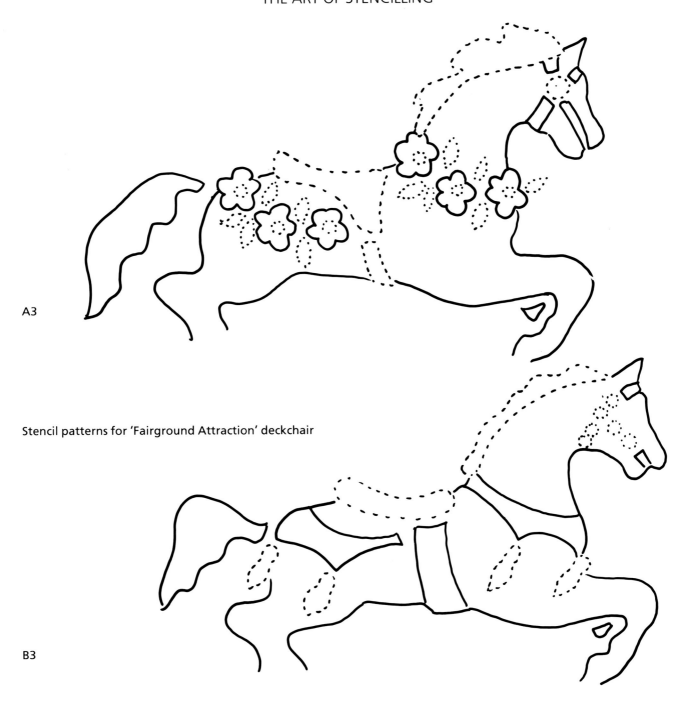

A3

Stencil patterns for 'Fairground Attraction' deckchair

B3

(*right*) KITES

Kites make an exciting subject for a child's room. Their simple, basic shape gives so much scope for flights of fancy everywhere from blinds and walls to lampshades and the bed. Use plain clear colours, as illustrated, for a bold effect: or more subtle shades, or draw just an outline, if you want to pattern the kites with decoration. The delicate curve of the tail, decorated with bows, adds just the right touch to soften the angular lines of the kite itself.

For this bedroom, the design is repeated on the rollerblind, lampshade and bed-head in strong primary colour combinations. The blind has the kites set against a blue sky, giving the room an outside aspect, even when the shades are drawn. Only the bows appear on the duvet, making it perfectly integrated without any danger of over-emphasising the design

In this case the kites are stencilled onto a painted wooden bed-head. But a plain straight or curved headboard could have a stencilled cover made from cotton sheeting.

The ribbon-like stripes on the wallpaper work well with the kites, echoing their drifting tails. But scattered kites could be flying freely across plain walls: or a more orderly frieze stencilled either halfway up, or bordering the top edge. And then there's always the ceiling, of course . . .

Design ideas for kite patterns

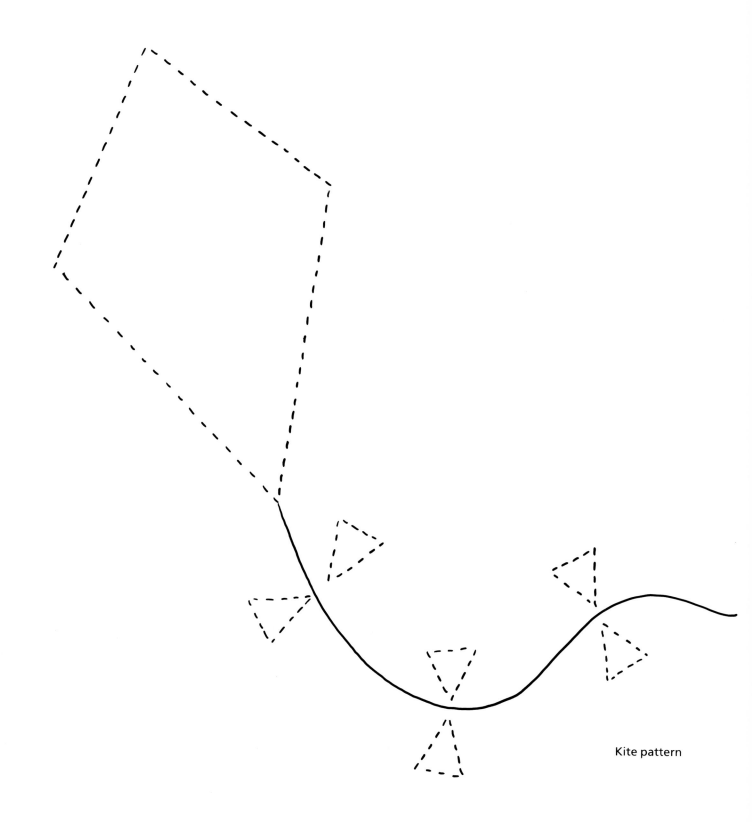

Kite pattern

CHAPTER 10

THE GUTTA-SERTI TECHNIQUE

Once again it was the Chinese who originally discovered and developed the art of using resist barriers in silk painting. Rice flour was mixed with other cereal ingredients to make a paste which was used to outline the design, forming tiny 'walls' which clogged the fibres of the woven mesh. When the area within the outline was painted, the colour was absorbed by the fabric and spread in the usual way – until it met the barrier, which resisted its movement and prevented it spreading further.

The Japanese used the technique extensively for kimono decoration. But it was not until the latter part of the sixteenth century that it found its way to Russia, reaching France and Italy in the early seventeenth century, where European textile artists greeted it with enthusiasm.

In order to work more detailed designs, much research and experiment was done with different compositions in an effort to find a superior type of 'resist' which would make a finer line than the rice paste or wax (another much used form of resist barrier). This eventually led to the development of the 'serti' technique, using a colourless rubber-based solution called gutta-percha. It is produced from certain trees native to Malaya, Borneo and Sumatra, either by refining the milky latex tapped from the tree itself, or by grinding and soaking the leaves to extract the gutta.

The Japanese had developed a technique for applying the rice paste by putting it into a paper cone, which was then squeezed to push a thin line of paste through a small hole made by cutting off the tip of the cone. The same method was successfully employed to draw the outline of the design with the waterproof rubber solution, gutta-percha.

The only disadvantage for the non-professional is the difficulty of removing the waterproof substance when the work is complete, since once the dyes are dry and fixed, the gutta has done its work. This has to be done by soaking the fabric in white spirit to remove the rubber base, which can be very dangerous if done near a naked flame or in a poorly ventilated room.

However, in recent years a water-based gutta has been developed, which can be removed by washing in a mild solution of soap and water, after the paints have been fixed by ironing. This type of gutta is produced by a number of different

'AQUARIUM' *by Sarah Lindsay*
The delicate and subtle use of silk paints to create this atmospheric painting demonstrates the infinite potential of the serti technique. The artist has used fine gutta outlines to give shape and form to the coral and seaweed on the ocean bed, then applied the paints in washes grading into solid blocks of colour.

There is a translucent and fluid quality about the whole composition of this exquisite underwater scene. The aqua-like serenity is given life and movement by a languid stream of small fish slowly weaving their way between the rocks and plants.

The work is also a perfect example of experienced colour mixing (Chapter 2). Sarah Lindsay has created the illusion of a wide spectrum of different colours: but study the picture carefully and you will identify only the primaries – blue, red and yellow – cleverly intermixed, and tinted with white, to create a harmonious range of soft shades

manufacturers: whichever you choose, it is very important to use paints of the same make.

Water-based gutta makes serti much easier and more enjoyable. And to simplify the drawing still more and give much greater control, this type of gutta is applied from a special bottle which is used as a 'pen', through a metal tip, which forms the 'nib'. These new developments also mean that serti is now safe for children, who find it specially exciting, because they can, for example, outline vivid colours with black to make 'stained glass windows', and produce similar vibrantly colourful effects.

Yet another revolutionary development has been the introduction of coloured and metallic gutta. These are even easier to use, because the colourless line is often difficult to see, once it has dried. But a black or coloured outline presents no problem at all. In fact, the metallic outliners provide yet another source of inspiration, because they can be used to considerable effect merely as a method of applying surface decoration, regardless of their barrier resist properties. The 'Argon Horse' appliqué bedspread illustrated here is a perfect example of a textile richly embellished with gold gutta.

The serti technique offers endless opportunities for exploration, as so many different effects can be achieved, especially when combined with other methods, like those in Chapter 6. A colourless outline will produce a delicate, stencil-like result, whilst a coloured or black one can give dramatic emphasis to a simple design, as in the 'Flowers in Ceramic' silk painting illustrated. Patience and care are more important than artistic talent, and the more practice you have, the more proficient you will become.

THE GUTTA-SERTI TECHNIQUE

Although serti is most effective on silk *fabrics*, it can also be used on others, such as wool crêpe and nunsveiling (lambswool) and fine, lightweight cottons. However, take extra care with these fabrics, and avoid using neutral (colourless) gutta, as it becomes almost invisible when it has dried.

Wash, dry and iron the fabric to remove any manufacturer's finish.

Use only *silk paints* for the serti technique: those used for the projects in this chapter are from the Deka-Silk range. And always use *gutta-percha outliners* made by the same manufacturer as your paint: Deka outliners were used here.

It is essential to have the silk stretched over a *frame* (see Chapter 3); make sure your fabric is large enough to allow a border for fixing to the frame with *three-pronged pins* (or silk pins) – or you can use *masking tape*.

The *gutta applicator* is a small pipette bottle, onto which you attach a special metal top which turns it into a pen. This section has a thin copper wire through it, which prevents the 'nib' becoming clogged with gutta while not in use: always replace it as soon as you finish drawing.

The *gutta pen* is available in several sizes, 5mm, 6mm and 8mm. The larger the size, the

Pipette bottle with cap

Snip off top of bottle with scissors before fixing the gutta pen (the wire prevents clogging when not in use)

Gutta pipette with pen attached: use masking tape to secure the pen to the bottle

thicker your line will be. Use *masking tape* to attach the pen top to the pipette bottle.

Although conventional brushes are perfectly suitable, they tend to wear out quickly, but special *silk painting brushes* last considerably longer: choose the size most appropriate to the area you are painting. *Cotton buds* are also ideal for applying paint, especially on detailed designs.

Coarse *sea salt* can often create exciting and attractive effects when used with serti (see Chapter 6).

Plastic *painting trays* with deep pans are ideal for silk paints. Alternatively, use *small china or plastic bowls or jars* to hold your paint. Have at least *two jars of water* in which to rinse your brushes: one for light colours and another for dark ones. *Face tissues* are useful to soak up excess paint on the fabric. Absorbent *paper towels* and/ or *soft rags* are essential to mop up excess paint and dry brushes.

You will also need the *appropriate materials* to prepare and transfer your designs, including a *black felt-tip pen.*

Drying may be speeded up with a hand-held *hair-dryer,* used on a medium heat setting (see below: step 9).

Cover your work surface and the immediate surroundings with a *plastic sheet* or *newspapers,* etc. Wear an *apron* or *overall,* and roll up your sleeves.

APPLICATION

1. Prepare your work-table, setting everything out ready for use. Select, but don't pour out the paints: have them standing in a shallow tray to avoid serious spillages if they are accidentally knocked over.
2. Draw or trace your design, and decide how you are going to transfer it to your fabric. If you are working on a very sheer silk, you may well find that, having drawn heavily over the outline on the tracing paper with a black felt-tip pen, you can see it through the fabric when it is placed underneath, close to – *but not touching* – the surface: a strong desk lamp above may help. Alternatively, a light box may be used for this purpose.

On the other hand, it may be necessary to transfer your design to the fabric using one of the other methods described in Chapter 4.
3. When all is ready, with your fabric stretched on the frame, the design in place, and the gutta pipette prepared, remove the wire from the pen section. Test the flow of gutta from the pipette on a piece of paper or scrap of fabric: when you apply slight pressure to the pipette, the gutta should run easily to draw an even line of the thickness that you require. It is important always to do this, because the larger pens sometimes dispense more fluid than expected, and also the coloured outliners tend to be more fluid than clear gutta.
4. When you are happy with the flow, hold the pen in your hand positioned at an angle as if you are going to write with a normal pen, above the fabric where you plan to begin drawing the design: if practical, it is a good idea to begin at the top left hand corner (or the right, if you are left-handed) and work down, to avoid smudging the lines you have already drawn.

Continue to apply slight pressure to the pipette and begin to draw in the outline of the design onto the fabric. Work slowly and carefully: hastily drawn lines may have breaks in them – which means certain disaster, as your 'barrier' will cease to 'resist' if there is a gap in it! Try to keep a steady pace without stopping and re-starting, as this will cause uneven lines, instead of the clean ones you are aiming for.

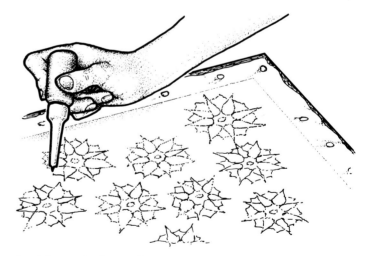

Applying gutta by tracing

5. When you have outlined the whole design, hold the framed fabric up against a window or other light source and check each line to see whether there are any breaks in the gutta: these gaps will form tiny outlets through which the paint will flow unhampered. So it is vitally important to spot them at this point and ensure that they are

(*above*) Applying gutta freehand, and (*below*) applying silk paint with a pointed brush

completely closed: apply the gutta pen very carefully to repair the break and join the line. You may find it worth checking the back of the fabric too, to make sure the gutta has penetrated the fibres sufficiently to block the mesh.

6. Leave the gutta until it is absolutely dry, preferably overnight.

7. Paint in the design between the outlined areas, using pointed brushes or a cotton bud. Begin at the centre of fairly small areas, like petals, and allow the paint to flow out to meet the gutta outline, working reasonably quickly to achieve an even spread of paint.

8. If you are planning a 'special effect' with salt (see Chapter 6), you must do this while the paint is still wet: as it dries quite quickly, have the salt ready and apply it as soon as you have finished painting the area.

9. Leave the paints until they are thoroughly dry.

If you use a hair-dryer, switch it to a medium heat and hold it about 15cm (6in) from the fabric: a higher heat, or holding it too close to the fabric, can cause scorch marks.

If you are working with heat-fixed paints, the use of a hair-dryer to aid drying will begin the fixing process. So, although you will still need to iron or oven-fix the paints, only half the usual time will be necessary.

10. If you have used salt, brush it all off very carefully.

11. Remove the fabric from the frame.

FIXING

If using the recommended paints (Deka-Silk), press the fabric on the wrong side for 3-5 minutes with a hot iron (*or* only half this time if you have used a hair-dryer: see step 9).

MINOR PROBLEMS AND HOW TO SOLVE THEM

BLOCKED PIPETTE This is the most common problem, caused by the gutta clogging the nib of the pen. Try to unblock it with the thin copper wire which comes with the pen. If this isn't successful, remove the pen from the pipette and wash it thoroughly in hot soapy water, soaking it for a while if necessary. Replace the pen and try again.

Remember always to replace the wire into the nib immediately after you have finished using the pen.

AIR BUBBLES If bubbles collect inside the pipette, unscrew the cap and squeeze the bottle: when a bubble comes to the surface, burst it with a pin. Repeat until all the bubbles have been dispersed.

SNAGGED FABRIC This probably means that your nib is worn, because the strong fibres of the silk are a harsh abrasive, and tend to damage the metal pen-nib. Renew your pen when you find the application is no longer smooth, or it begins to snag the fabric.

LEAKING PEN You may not have used the best tape to attach the pen to the pipette. Masking tape is the first choice, or you can use insulating tape, but ordinary clear adhesive tape is not suitable, as it allows the gutta to leak through at the bottom of the pen, which can become very messy.

IRREGULAR FLOW The gutta may thicken, preventing it from flowing smoothly through the nib. This could be caused simply by the gutta being too cold: in which case, a few hours at room temperature should return it to its normal consistency.

However, the gutta may also thicken with age – or because the bottle has not been properly re-sealed. If this happens, the consistency of the gutta can be corrected by adding a thinner, one drop at a time: shake and check after each drop, until the flow is right for working. The solvent or thinner will depend on the type of gutta you are using, so check the product.

SMUDGED LINES Take care to avoid touching the gutta line once it is drawn, because it remains sticky for some time. Also, wipe the nib with a tissue from time to time, to prevent a build-up of thickening gutta around the tip.

GUTTA REMAINS ON THE SURFACE If the gutta does not penetrate the fabric properly, it may be because it is too thick. If this is the case, thin it as above. Or it may be that the fabric itself is too thick. In this case, draw another gutta line on the back of the fabric, directly under the first one.

PUDDLES Take care not to use silk paint over-generously: if you apply too much it will form a puddle, and subsequently drip through the fine fabric onto your work-surface, or the design beneath. If the wet fabric then sags down and touches the paint below, you will have unsightly marks and patches. Avoid overloading your brush, and if any puddles do appear, quickly blot them up by gently dabbing with a face tissue, or holding a dry paintbrush on top to absorb the excess paint.

SAGGING FABRIC If the weight of the wet paint causes the fabric to sag, you will be in danger of it touching the work-surface below. Try to avoid using too much paint, and blot puddles with a face tissue (see previous paragraph). If you are still worried, it may be necessary to tighten up the pins to make the fabric taut again – raising the frame as a precaution whilst you do so.

PAINT SEEPING THROUGH THE BARRIER No matter how careful you are, there are occasions when small 'bridges' occur in the outline because the gutta has not penetrated the fibres of the fabric: these cannot be seen when you check for gaps. When this happens, the paint will seep through and spread over the fabric on the other side of the line. Your first move is to hold a dry cotton bud, or a brush, over the bleeding paint, to soak up the excess and stop the flow. If the leak is only a small one, there is no need to worry, as it shouldn't distract from the overall design when the work is finished.

However, if the escape is more serious, and spoils the appearance of the design, there are various measures you might consider taking to disguise it.

a. Could you pretend that you planned a salt effect in this area? Sprinkle salt over the bleeding paint and the surrounding fabric: when all the paint has moved about, the intruder will be much less obvious. But you will probably have to invent some other 'salted' areas, to balance the design. Just one small patch might look a little odd!

b. Would it be possible to extend the area of colour? Try adding something on at that point: another petal, a leaf, even a small 'doodle' – using your gutta outliner to make it look like part of the original design. It need not even be the same colour: you could paint over the leak in a darker colour.

c. Perhaps you could make the leak itself look intentional? Very carefully paint just enough colour against the gutta line on either side of the leak, to create a softly blurred edge to the whole line, instead of in only one place. This often works very well, and can look most attractive.

d. Or might you be able to change your original plans and paint the adjoining area also in the bleeding colour? Or else in a darker colour, taking in the leak as well – which may still show as a slight shadow, but shouldn't be too obtrusive. However, if you try to paint over it with a lighter colour, the leak will remain just as obvious.

NOTE: Remember to repair the gutta line (if necessary from underneath) before you try to remedy the problem. Otherwise any paint you apply on the leaked side will bleed through to the side that you painted originally, and you will have the same problem in reverse!

THE 'TRIPOLI' CUSHIONS

A trio of cushions which have a lot to say about design, as well as the serti technique. Three quite different designs produce three cushions, each of which would make a strong impact used independently in a single setting. But bring them together on a sofa or window-seat, and you have a perfectly co-ordinated piece of design.

You could use a neutral gutta, or outline the shapes in black or in colour rather than the gold shown here.

Your *painting fabric* is three squares of Habotai silk 8 or 12mm (see Workshop Section) large enough to cover the cushion pads of your choice (see below) PLUS a border allowance of 2.5cm (1in) all round. You will also need three squares of *backing fabric* the same size as the pad PLUS a 1.5cm (⅝in) seam allowance. You may need a *lining fabric* to back the silk: this can be the same as the backs.

Three standard size *cushion pads*: these may be 40cm (16in), 45cm (18in), 50cm (20in) or 55cm (22in) square.

It is essential to use *silk paints*. These are Deka-Silk in Bordo, Ultramarine and Yellow.

A *gold gutta outliner* was used, for which you will need a *gutta bottle or pipette* and a *6mm gutta pen*.

Have a *frame* to fit your silk squares (see Chapter 3), together with *three-pronged pins* or silk pins (Chapter 3).

You will also require all the *usual materials* for drawing and transferring the design (Chapter 4) and the general *painting equipment*.

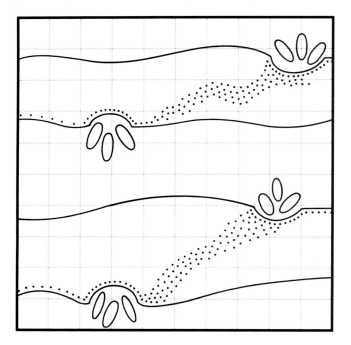

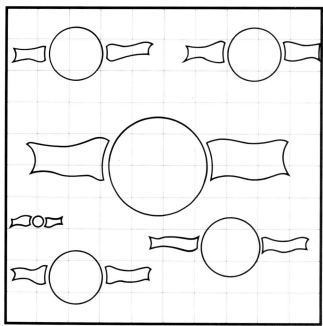

Tripoli cushion patterns

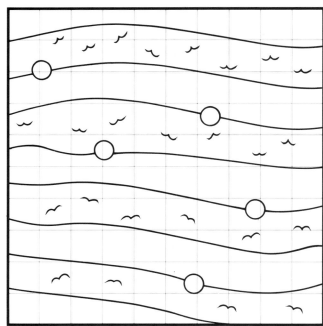

(*right*) The vibrant 'Tripoli' cushions; gutta-serti on silk

APPLICATION

1. On a sheet of paper, rule a square outline to the finished measurement of your cushion (as governed by the pad). Divide it into equal squares, ten in each direction, then draw out your pattern using the Grid System, as directed in Chapter 4. Go over the whole design with a black felt-tip pen to make a heavy outline.
   Repeat for each design.
2. Rule a square on one piece of silk, to indicate the finished size of your cushion, allowing an equal surplus all round. Then stretch it over your frame, pinning it so that it is taut and even (see Chapter 3).
3. Place the design under your fabric to check whether you can see it clearly enough to trace your gutta outline, as explained in the basic directions: step 2. If not, use one of the methods suggested in Chapter 4 to transfer the design to your fabric, using the most suitable marker.
4. Draw over all the lines of the design with your gutta outliner, using the pen as described in the basic directions: steps 3 and 4.
5. Hold your frame up against a window or other strong light source and check very carefully for gaps or breaks in the gutta lines. If you see any, repair them by applying more

gutta, if necessary from the back (basic directions: step 5).
6. Allow the gutta to dry thoroughly, ideally overnight.
7. Prepare your paints. Then, following the illustration for guidance, paint the design as described in the basic directions: step 7.
8. Leave until the paint is completely dry (using a hair dryer, if you wish, as directed: step 9). Don't leave in direct sunlight, or the colours may fade.
9. Remove the silk from the frame, and repeat for the other two cushions.

FIXING

If using the recommended Deka-Silk paints, press the fabric on the wrong side for 3-5 minutes (half this time if you have used a hair dryer), with a steam iron. For other paints, follow the manufacturer's instructions.

MAKING UP THE TRIPOLI CUSHIONS

1. If it is necessary to line the painted fabric, place the right side of the lining fabric behind the silk and pin them together, making sure they are both absolutely flat. Then, using matching thread, tack them together along the lines indicating the finished edge of the cushion.
   If you are not lining the cushion, either stitch along this line in the same way, or else mark it clearly on the back of the silk.
2. Pin the cushion front to the backing fabric, right sides together. Then stitch along the marked line, leaving a gap at one side large enough to insert the cushion pad.
3. Trim the seams and mitre the corners (cut them off diagonally, fairly close to the stitches).
4. Turn to the right side and push out the seams, tacking to hold them in place if necessary. Then press.
5. Insert the cushion pad, slip-stitching the edges of the opening neatly together afterwards.

(*right*) KIMONO WALLHANGING
This splendid kimono, painted in vibrant silk colours, makes an unusual – but spectacularly effective – wall decoration. If you insist on authenticity, make up a commercial pattern for an adult kimono. But if you prefer the easy option, simply follow the lines of the diagram (page 104), scaling it up to the size required (see Chapter 4), to make a kimono-shaped flat wallhanging.

Use a heavy Habotai silk, and outline the pattern with clear gutta before painting the fabric with glowing silk colours, spaced out with just enough black to emphasise the brilliant colours still further. The finishing touches are worked with black and gold gutta outliners.

Your colour scheme can be any exciting combination of paints that in your own imagination suggests the Orient: but for the greatest effect, restrict the number you use. The dramatic impact of this kimono relies on the use of only three almost translucent jewel colours: deep sapphire, ruby and amber

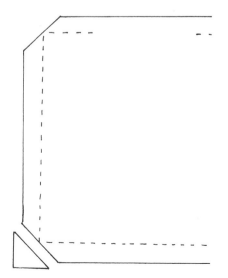

Mitre the corners

Alison Hob

THE KIMONO CUSHION

The classically simple shape of the kimono inspires a fascinating cushion with the strong motif picked out in bold colours. Contrasting straight and curled lines are added to produce a well-balanced, but nevertheless very striking design.

You will need a square of *Habotai silk, backing fabric, lining fabric* (if required) and a *cushion pad*: for full details of all these, see the Tripoli cushions.

You will require *silk paints* in black, true red and yellow (these are Deka-Silk and a *neutral (colourless) gutta outliner,* together with a *gutta bottle or pipette* and a *6mm gutta pen.*

Also a *frame, pins* and all the *other materials* and *painting equipment* described for the Tripoli cushions.

For application, fixing and making up the kimono cushion, follow the directions for the Tripoli cushions.

Kimono cushion pattern

(*right*) The kimono cushion – a strong motif picked out in bold colours on silk

THE TURKEYSTAN CUSHION

The warm colours of the Middle East are intensified by using a cream coloured Antung silk, which has the effect of deepening them to shades of even greater strength and subtlety. The rich colours are emphasised and enhanced by the resist barriers of gold gutta used to draw the pattern of gilded horizontal, vertical and diagonal lines which compose the design.

You will need a square of *Antung silk, backing fabric, lining fabric* (if required) and a *cushion pad:* for full details, see the Tripoli cushions.

You will require *silk paints* in ultramarine, sienna and ochre (these are Deka-Silk) and a *gold gutta outliner,* together with a *gutta bottle or pipette* and a *6mm gutta pen.*

Also a *frame, pins* and all the *other materials* and *painting equipment* described for the Tripoli cushions.

For application, fixing and making up, follow the directions for the Tripoli cushions.

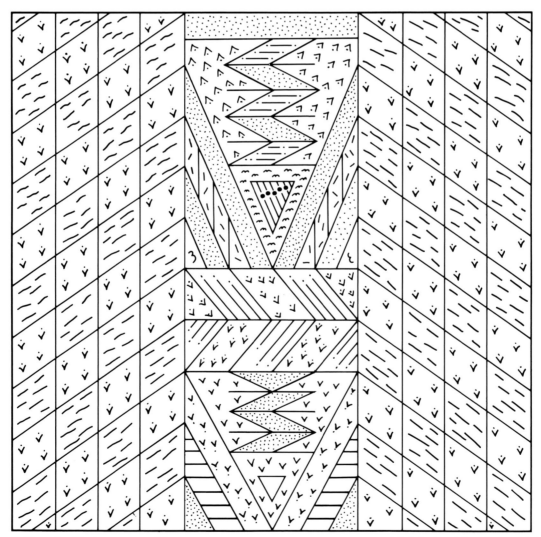

Pattern for Turkeystan cushion

(*right*) The rich colours of the Turkeystan cushion are enhanced by the use of cream-coloured Antung silk

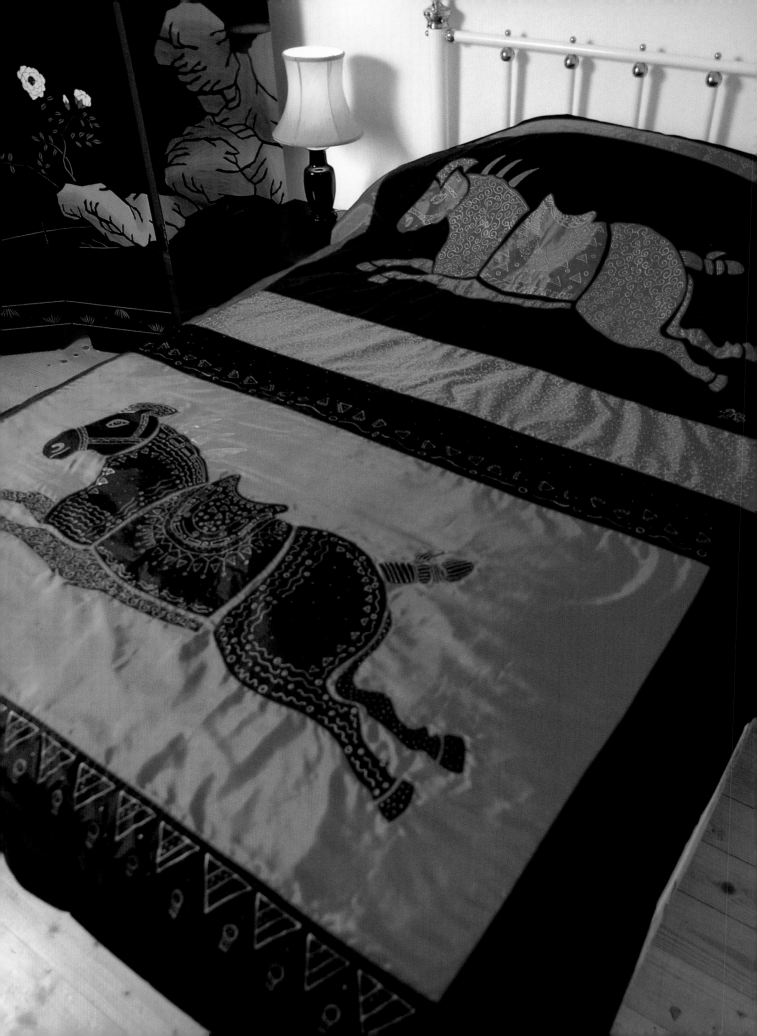

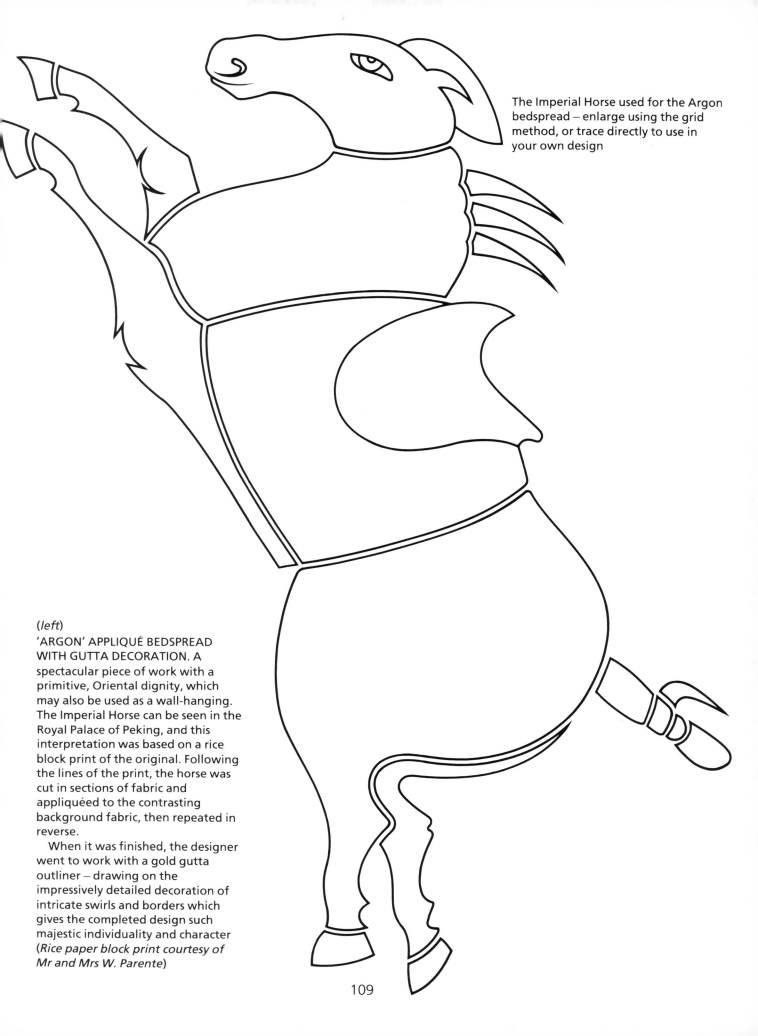

The Imperial Horse used for the Argon bedspread – enlarge using the grid method, or trace directly to use in your own design

(*left*)
'ARGON' APPLIQUÉ BEDSPREAD WITH GUTTA DECORATION. A spectacular piece of work with a primitive, Oriental dignity, which may also be used as a wall-hanging. The Imperial Horse can be seen in the Royal Palace of Peking, and this interpretation was based on a rice block print of the original. Following the lines of the print, the horse was cut in sections of fabric and appliquéed to the contrasting background fabric, then repeated in reverse.

When it was finished, the designer went to work with a gold gutta outliner – drawing on the impressively detailed decoration of intricate swirls and borders which gives the completed design such majestic individuality and character (*Rice paper block print courtesy of Mr and Mrs W. Parente*)

Two inspirational spiral designs by Paul Sparling. They were drawn on paper with compasses, then traced onto cloth with gutta and painted in with silk paints

CHAPTER 11

THE ANCIENT CRAFT OF BATIK

The romantic islands of Java and Bali are the traditional homes of the fascinating art of batik. Like the serti technique, a 'resist barrier' is used to prevent colour penetrating those areas where it is not wanted: but in this case the resist is wax. The craft has been practised in the Indonesian islands since the eighth century (having been brought from China), and its unique charm gradually spread to make this richly coloured form of textile decoration popular all over the world.

Usually worked on fine, soft cotton, liquid wax is used to cover certain areas of the design. If the cloth is white, the waxed areas will remain white: if it is coloured, that colour will be preserved. The fabric is then immersed in a bath of, for instance, yellow dye: on white cotton, all the unwaxed areas will now be yellow. When the fabric is dry, more wax is applied, this time over certain parts of the design in the yellow area. Once more the cotton is dyed: this time it might be red. All the wax-covered white and yellow areas will remain: the clear fabric will be red. The whole process might be repeated again, with some of the red area of the design now being covered with wax before the cloth is dipped a third time, perhaps in brown dye. Then the wax is removed, leaving traditional designs, often representing Indonesian life, natural history and dance, in warm glowing colour.

Another attractive characteristic of batik, which makes the primitive designs even more instantly recognisable, is the unusual 'cracked' effect over the whole, or part of the fabric. This is created by

Examples of Indonesian batik

painting the cotton with brittle wax and, when it is hard, actually cracking it by crumpling the cloth. Then it is dyed again, so that the dye penetrates between the hairline cracks, and the tiny veined lines appear across the design.

Interesting as it is to admire and study, batik has definite disadvantages compared to the modern serti method of barrier resist. The continual dyeing makes it a lengthy process, and also means that the fabric has to be repeatedly pinned to, and removed from, the frame. The hot wax must of course be handled with care, and can present a safety hazard if children are likely to be around because the paraffin content makes it highly inflammable, and could also cause toxic fumes. And the removal of the wax can be rather tedious.

So if you are simply looking for an efficient barrier resist, you would do well to confine yourself to serti. But if you are tempted to experiment with batik, you could 'cheat' a little in order to avoid several time-consuming operations – although by no means all the drawbacks are eliminated. Fabric paints can be used to do the work of the dyes, to create an effect very similar to batik: this allows the fabric to remain on the frame through each process, until it is almost finished. This is variously known as 'imitation batik', 'false batik' or 'faux batik'.

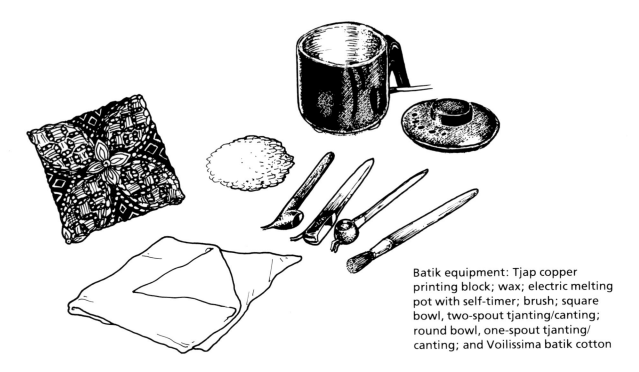

Batik equipment: Tjap copper printing block; wax; electric melting pot with self-timer; brush; square bowl, two-spout tjanting/canting; round bowl, one-spout tjanting/canting; and Voilissima batik cotton

THE BATIK WAX RESIST TECHNIQUE

The traditional, and best, *fabric* to use for batik is cotton. Two of the most popular cottons, ideal for this purpose because of their exceptionally smooth surface and strong, yet yielding texture, are *Voilissima* and *Primissima*. Cotton *lawn* is a suitable alternative. Silk and wool may also be used, but both have to be handled carefully: silk will absorb the wax far more quickly than cotton, whilst wool soaks it up more slowly because of its own natural oil content.

There are various *paints and dyes* on the market which are recommended for batik. Choose the type which appeals to you most for the method and fabric you are using. However, if you are working on the kind of fine cotton suggested, silk paints should produce very successful results (as for serti: see previous chapter).

A *melting pot* is necessary to heat the wax. Although a special, thermostatically controlled pot is the ideal, you will probably not wish to purchase such an expensive piece of equipment for your first experiments. A small pan makes an adequate alternative: but it should *never* be used over a naked flame. An electric stove or hotplate should always be used.

A *frame* is highly recommended, if not essential (see Chapter 3), as for the serti technique.

The *application* of the melted wax may be done in various ways. The traditional Indonesian tool is the *tjanting*. The hot wax is held in a small copper bowl, fixed to a wooden or bamboo handle: a tiny spout, like a miniature teapot, allows a steady flow of molten wax to pour out of the bowl onto the fabric. The bowls come in several different shapes, and the spouts will differ in size according to the thickness of the line you wish to draw: you can even have two or more spouts. But whatever the tjanting/canting looks like, the basic principle remains the same.

To cover larger areas of fabric, paint the wax on with a *brush*, choosing one with man-made

Applying the wax

bristles, which are more durable than natural hair. It is necessary to work quickly when applying wax with a brush, as it cools rapidly and builds up in the bristles: dip the brush into the hot wax frequently to prevent this happening. Nevertheless, interesting textures can be achieved by drawing the stiff bristles over partially hardened wax as it cools.

A pad of *cotton wool* may also be used, or, for small areas, *cotton buds* can be useful: both these avoid the problem of cooling wax clogging the bristles of a brush.

Another much-used traditional method is the *tjap*, which is a special block used for printing the typical Indonesian repeat designs onto the fabric. The face of the block is made up of long copper strips which are cut up and bent into shapes which are then soldered to a metal base to form the design. The block has a handle at the back, which is bound with strips of cloth to protect the printer's hand from the intense heat of the metal when the block is dipped in the hot wax. The tjap is either pressed onto a pad which has been soaked with wax, or else dipped into a shallow tray of hot wax, where it is left long enough to adapt to the temperature, then removed and tapped to release the excess. The waxed block is pressed firmly down onto the fabric, where it leaves an accurate impression. The same procedure is followed over and over again, carefully matched edge-to-edge, to produce a repeat design.

Scrunched up *rags* dipped in molten wax can produce interesting background effects and textures. So can *sticks* and other improvised tools when used to apply the wax.

When using the tjanting, a *stopper* is necessary to prevent the wax being released when it is not actually in use. This can be a *cork:* but it is usually easier to hold a *soft rag, pad of cotton wool*, absorbent *paper towel, man-size paper handkerchief* or *face tissue* in your other hand, as these are useful to wipe the spout free of congealing wax and catch drips.

Another *large rag* should also be close at hand for cleaning the hands and mopping up excess or spilled wax from surfaces and equipment.

If the wax cools down too much in the bowl of the tjanting, it may solidify in the spout. If this happens, use a *fine wire* to clear the blockage.

The most important item is, of course, the *wax*.

In Javanese and Balinese families their wax recipes were a close-kept secret, as were the composition of their dyes. But modern batik holds no mysteries: the wax is readily available from craft shops and candlemakers' suppliers. It can be bought in blocks, candles or granules, and is a combination of beeswax and paraffin wax – in varying proportions which are determined by the purpose for which it is required. For drawing, a soft wax is needed: 40% beeswax and 60% paraffin wax (or four parts beeswax to six parts paraffin wax). If the ratio of paraffin wax is too high, the hardened wax will crack and flake off the fabric. But for the 'cracked' effect, a more brittle wax is needed: 30% beeswax and 70% paraffin wax (or three parts beeswax to seven parts paraffin wax). It is also possible to buy special ready-prepared batik wax.

The blocks, candles or granules are melted down to a clear liquid, which is usually reached approaching or about 136°F (58°C). As already pointed out, this should not be done over a naked flame: if you haven't access to a thermostatically controlled wax pot, use a steel or aluminium pan, preferably without any special non-stick coating. Watch the melting wax very carefully to avoid overheating, and remove the pan immediately if there is any sign of smoke: the fumes can be dangerous. If fire should occur through overheating, turn off the heat immediately and smother the flames with a damp cloth, a large pan lid or bicarbonate of soda.

The molten wax may be retained at the correct temperature if the pan is placed in a larger pan or baking tin of hot water – just like the *bain marie* much used in Victorian kitchens to cook sauces and keep other small items hot. The pan or tin must be somewhat bigger than the pan of wax, and should be one-third filled with water. Heat the water until it comes almost to the boil, then place the pan of wax in the larger pan, taking care not to let any water splash into the wax. Keep the water near boiling point, but don't allow it to boil: this will keep your wax to the same even consistency for as long as you need it (don't forget to top up the hot water when necessary!).

The wax is reconstituted as it cools down, but it can be recycled several times. However, make sure there are no impurities left when you are using the wax again, because any small foreign bodies could disfigure your work. Strain the wax

Two pieces by the highly regarded batik artist, Noel Dyrenforth, whose work has been exhibited all over the world. 'Island' can be seen at the Victoria and Albert Museum, London. 'Fallen Idol' is in a private collection

through a *cloth or a fine mesh metal strainer,* heating it sufficiently so that it pours through easily.

Plenty of *absorbent paper* (brown wrapping paper, lining paper, kitchen towels, etc) is necessary to remove the wax from the fabric, which is melted with a hot *dry iron.*

NOTE: It is wise not to use a *hair dryer* to speed drying, as it could melt the hardened wax barriers.

APPLICATION: USING THE TJANTING FOR TULIS WORK

Tulis work is the traditional method of drawing with wax, which is used by the Indonesians to create the intricate designs which make true batik so instantly recognisable.

1. Wash and press the fabric (note any manufacturer's instructions on the product, if you are using special dyes).
2. Draw out your design on the fabric, using the most suitable method and marker (Chapter 4).
3. Stretch and pin the fabric over your frame (Chapter 3).
4. Prepare the wax, as already described. Place it close to hand so that it is easily reached for re-filling (turn handles away from you to prevent accidents).
5. When it has reached the right temperature and consistency, dip the bowl of the tjanting into the

wax and leave it for a few seconds for the metal to absorb the heat. Then lift it out and immediately tilt it backwards very carefully, holding a paper towel, tissue, soft rag or pad of cotton wool over the spout to stop the wax running out, wiping the bowl at the same time to prevent drips. As you work, check underneath the bowl frequently, and wipe away any dripping wax.

6. Holding the tjanting quite close to the fabric, release the stopper and start drawing straight away, as the wax will begin to flow immediately. It is advisable to do a 'test run' on a spare piece of cloth before you begin work on your proposed design, as learning to control the tjanting whilst you are drawing takes a certain amount of patience and skill. You are aiming for a long, thin,

regular line. If the wax is too hot, it will spread and leave an uneven line: let it cool a little before continuing. On the other hand, if the wax doesn't flow easily, it means that it is not hot enough: return the tjanting to the pan and allow the bowl to adjust fully to the temperature of the wax.

7. When you have finished drawing out your design in wax, and it is quite dry, turn the fabric over to make sure the wax has penetrated the cloth fully. If it hasn't, repeat the design directly behind the first application of wax. You can also make the design more interesting by drawing another, interlacing pattern on the back.

8. Fill in any large resist areas with a brush, working as quickly as possible to prevent the cooling wax building up in the bristles. Stencils

may be used as templates when applying wax with a brush (Stencilling: Chapter 9).

9. This type of hand-drawn batik work can be either dyed or hand-painted, using the dyes or paints as instructed.

Coarse sea salt may be added to create yet another effect, or the paint could be sponged on (see Chapter 6).

APPLICATION: WITH OR WITHOUT CERNÉ

Cerné is similar to serti, but uses wax and a tjanting instead of gutta and a pen. As for serti, silk paints are recommended.

1. Prepare your fabric, design and wax as steps 1-5 above.

2. Follow the tjanting directions in step 6, but use it to outline areas of the design as described in the previous chapter (these lines will remain white – or the original basic colour of the fabric). When the wax has hardened, apply your colours in the same way as for serti, using the wax barriers to resist the spreading paint.

The alternative to cerné, which entails applying your different paint colours one-by-one between separate waxings, is closer to the methods of true batik. First plan the colour scheme for your design, so that you can work out the order in

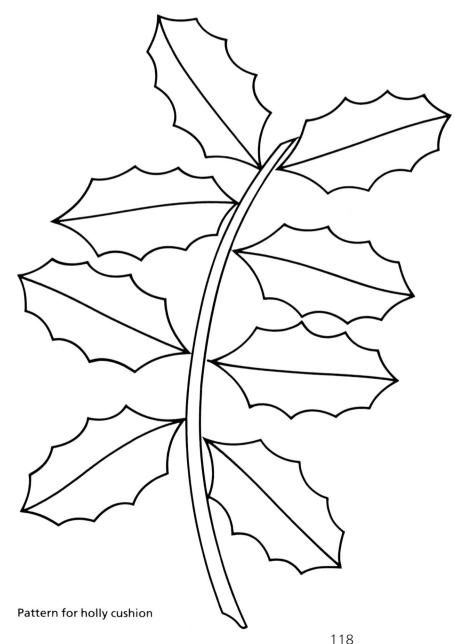

(right)
This very attractive small cushion takes a traditional Western theme for its design – interpreted with all the charm of true batik. The holly leaf design can be used individually all over the cushion, or formed into a branch as illustrated.

It was first traced onto paper with a heavy outline, then traced onto the fabric – which can be silk, or as in this case, sheer cotton – using a very light coloured pencil. When the fabric had been stretched on a frame, the design was outlined with a medium size tjanting filled with drawing wax. Then brittle wax was brushed all round the design, covering the whole outside area.

The wax was left until it was completely dry. Then, without disturbing the line of the holly leaves, the brittle wax was cracked by scrunching it with the fingers until fine lines appeared all over it. The fabric was then soaked in a medium green dye bath. After removal from the dye, it was rinsed and left to dry before the wax was removed as described above. The cushion was made up with lines of quilting stitches emphasising the stems, and crimson beads sewn on for the berries

Pattern for holly cushion

which you will need to apply your paints, beginning with the lightest (ie yellow), and working through to the darkest (ie brown or black). You can have as many colours as you like, but don't forget that one colour over another may produce something quite different: so it's a good idea to test the colours you plan to use, laying one over another in the order in which you plan to apply them.

1. Prepare your fabric, design and wax as for the tjanting (see above).
2. Use your tjanting as directed in step 6, or a brush etc, to cover only those areas which you want to remain the colour of your fabric.
3. When the wax has hardened, paint the unwaxed areas, beginning with the lightest colour, ie yellow.
4. When the paint is quite dry, apply more wax – this time covering those areas which you wish to remain yellow.
5. When the wax is hard, paint the fabric again, in a slightly stronger colour, ie red.
6. Continue these two processes until you have built up all the colours of your design in wax resist, as described in the opening paragraphs of this chapter.

APPLICATION: THE CRACKING EFFECT

Purists sometimes frown at the random lines of delicate veined 'cracks' resembling marble, which so often appear over the traditional designs. But lovers of batik consider it is an essential feature, and one of its greatest attractions.

As mentioned previously, a special 'brittle' wax is necessary (30% beeswax to 70% paraffin wax), which is much harder and apt to break and crack very easily. This is prepared in the usual way, and when it is the correct consistency, a thin layer is brushed all over the fabric and allowed to dry. To increase the effect, you can, if you wish, turn the fabric over and brush another thin layer of wax over the back. When the wax is completely dry and hard, the fabric is removed from the frame and crumpled in the hands: controlled cracks can be made by folding or pleating the cloth in certain directions only.

The fabric is then laid flat on the covered work surface, or re-pinned to the frame, and brushed all over with paint in a darker colour, so that it penetrates the cracks in the wax.

REMOVING THE WAX

There are various methods (all rather tedious, unfortunately!) for removing the wax. Cotton may be boiled until all the wax has dislodged from the fibres and risen to the surface so that it can be skimmed off: then it has to be washed very carefully. Sometimes the wax can be scraped off, using a broad blade. Or the fabric can be ironed between sheets of absorbent paper (use a hot dry iron, not a steam one) renewing the paper repeatedly as it soaks up the wax, until it has all been absorbed. This is the one most commonly recommended.

On the other hand, there are certain special removal fluids which your artist's materials or batik supplier will be able to tell you about.

CLEANING AND CARING FOR YOUR EQUIPMENT

Place your utensils, tjantings, brushes, etc in a large pan of boiling water and add a cupful of soda crystals. Mix well and leave to boil for several minutes, or until you see a wax skin forming on the surface.

Leave the pan alone until the water is cold, when the wax should have formed a thick layer on the surface. Remove the congealed wax. Repeat and skim again if necessary.

After boiling, wash brushes in a mild solution of fabric conditioner to keep the bristles soft. Dry all utensils and equipment thoroughly with a soft cloth before storing.

Scrape and clean your iron very thoroughly after use, to remove any remaining wax.

(*right and overleaf*) Batik patterns taken from Indonesian textiles

(*right*)
DELFT BLUE ROCKING CHAIR WITH RUNNER
A homely wicker basket filled with colourful balls of wool completes this scene of cosy domesticity and gentle relaxation. The rush seat of the wooden-frame rocking chair is treated to a long cushion runner which combines restful comfort with style and good looks. Even the teacups decorating each section of the padded cushion are a comfortable shape, and everything combines to create an atmosphere evocative of a Dutch interior painted by an old master.

The textile design is a superb example of 'imitation' or 'false' batik, using just one colour – a glorious Delft blue matched to the wall plates and flower jug – on a white ground. The wax resist barriers were painted in with a brush, but for greater detail, they could be drawn with a tjanting/canting. Alternatively, if you want to avoid using wax, you can create exactly the same effect with gutta, using the serti technique. For either method, silk paint works well on the fine cotton.

The five lightly padded cushions could be made up separately and joined, or the whole runner could be made from one long length of batiked fabric, with separate layers of wadding behind each section of the design. Another complete length of wadding is sandwiched between the front and back before they are sewn together. Then the runner is stitched between each design repeat to divide the cushions, with more stitching quilting the edges. Just for fun, the generously shaped cups might be quilted, too. The runner is fastened to the chair with narrow ties at the top and back of the seat.

This warmly inviting decor demonstrates to perfection how to avoid any suggestion of coldness in a blue colour scheme. Having been used for the main subject, it is surrounded by softly muted peaches and yellow which harmonise with the chair itself, with only small echoing touches of blue repeated elsewhere (see Colour in the Home: Chapter 16)

CHAPTER 12

THE BEAUTY OF MARBLING

The technique of marbling was discovered by the Japanese many hundreds of years ago, where it was called suminagashi, and was a favourite art form to decorate sheets of poetry. It still enjoys great popularity, both as an individual craft, and also used commercially for textiles. From Japan it reached the Middle East: Sir Francis Bacon, writing in 1627, was impressed by the method used by the Turks to decorate paper with oil paints, and Sir Thomas Herbert encountered it in his travels in Persia in the same year. Travelling artisans introduced it to Europe, where for centuries the only way to decorate paper had been by laborious hand-painting.

This incredibly effective process must have seemed like near-magic to European artists, who were enchanted with the new craft and took it to their hearts immediately. Marbling soon became an important industry in France and Germany, where it was much used in bookbinding and also to line cupboards, chests and boxes, and for mirror-backs. Italy and Spain also produced much beautiful work. It was some time before the technique eventually reached England, but by the mid nineteenth century the craft had declined in France and Germany, whilst the work of English marbling artists excelled. Many artistic designs developed down the centuries, known by such evocative names as French Shell, Marble Cut and Peacock Curl.

In principle, the technique of marbling paper is amazingly simple. A large, shallow tray of 'size' is made up (imagine a large baking tin filled with thick wallpaper paste). Different colour oil paints are dropped onto the surface of the size and, if it is the right consistency, they will float and form a thin skin. The colours are then gently swirled about with a pin or a thin stick to form an attractive pattern: this happens because the paints repel one another and retain their individual colours instead of mixing together. Then the paper is laid gently on top – and lifted off again, bringing the 'skin' of paint with it.

Although the basic method is in itself relatively easy, the success of marbling relies entirely on correct and careful preparation of the size materials. The traditional paints were water colours, prepared from finely ground pigments to which ox gall was added to make them spread. An easier alternative is to use oil paints, but the results are not so fine. Special paints are now available, but the consistency of the size is still the most important element: it must be sufficiently thin to allow the paints to move about, whilst being thick enough to hold them on the surface without sinking. The best way to perfect the method yourself is by trial and error, so follow the directions and experiment freely on sheets of paper before trying it out on fabric.

Marbling fabric, instead of paper, was an obvious extension of the technique, but this presented problems. However, over the past decade colour chemists have been hard at work developing suitable paints, which are water-based and washable, specifically for marbling textiles. The results are now available in a range of easy-to-use paints which achieve fascinating results – excitingly different every time.

THE MARBLING TECHNIQUE

The best effects are achieved on cotton and silk *fabrics:* but it is important to adapt the size to suit the fabric. For *silk,* you will need a medium-

There are so many elegant uses for marbled fabrics. But covered stationery must be one of the most effective. Here a plain notebook and pencil show how attractive a marbled design can be when it is used for this purpose. The smart little boxes might be especially suitable to hold small gifts for a man, whilst every keen reader would welcome the simple bookmark (*Marbled fabrics by Judith Perry*)

thick size, but for *cotton*, the mixture should be slightly thicker.

There are several different types of *marbling paints* on the market: some are still partially oil-based, whilst others are totally water-based. Dryatt and Hobbidee are two brands which can be recommended.

Oil-based batik paints or other *oil paints* may be used, diluted with turpentine. However, although they are colour-fast once they have dried on the fabric, when the paint is floated on the size the oil content separates to form small globules: this causes the pattern you have created to stay in position for only a very short time, so it is essential to work fast.

The size has to be floated in a *plastic tray* which is large enough to accommodate the piece of fabric you plan to marble. It must be at least 5cm (2in) deep. Plastic seed trays, photograph development trays or cat litter trays all do the job very well, and are available in several sizes: 50 x 60cm (20 x 25in) is a practical choice. For larger pieces of fabric, children's plastic sand and water trays, from toy shops, are ideal.

The size must be strained through a *coarse nylon sieve* or a *muslin cloth* to free it from lumps and to achieve a perfectly smooth mixture.

The paint is dropped onto the size with a *drop brush* or *pipette*. Wooden sticks are also suitable for this purpose, as well as for mixing paint and pulling the floated colours into a marbled pattern: *wooden skewers, nail manicure orange sticks* and *wooden cocktail sticks* are all useful.

Beautiful patterns can be formed by drawing a *comb* over the floating paint. Special pattern combs may be purchased from marbling suppliers –or you can make your own. (See Figures 1, 2, 3 and 4.)

A cold water size should be made up in a *plastic bucket:* use one that will hold at least 10 litres (10 quarts) of water, so that you have plenty of room to mix the size.

A size which needs to be boiled should be made in a *large saucepan:* this again needs to be big enough to allow the size to be mixed comfortably.

A *wooden spoon* or *stick* is needed to stir the size in the bucket or pan.

Also a *whisk* for mixing – electric or hand-operated.

Place your paints on *small deep dishes*, which you can also use for mixing.

Dropping paint onto the size with a pipette bottle

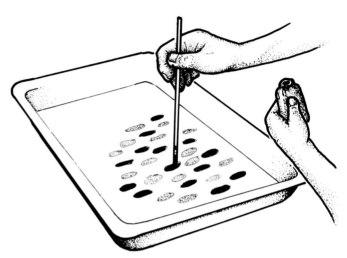

Dropping paint onto the size with a drop stick: the stick is dipped into the paint, then held over the size to allow droplets of paint to run down and fall onto the surface

Using a stick to draw the paint into swirls

Unless they are specifically intended for marbling on cloth, oil-based paints should be diluted with *turpentine*, which you will also require for cleaning your equipment. (Work in a well-ventilated place, away from any naked flame,

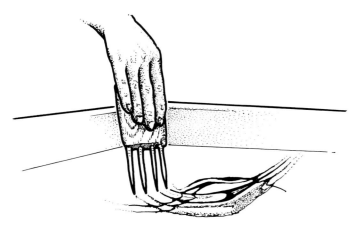

Using a four-toothed nail comb

Laying the fabric on the patterned surface of the size

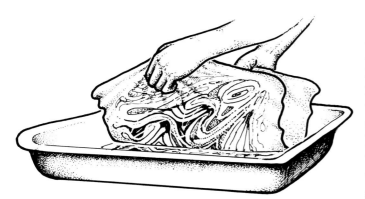

Lifting the fabric off the size in one movement

when using turps or white spirit.)

Do not dilute water-based paints, as it weakens their adhering properties.

The freshly marbled fabric is laid out flat on *old newspapers* to dry, as hanging might allow the

paint to continue running, and distort the pattern.

You have a choice of methods and recipes to make up the all-important *size* for the base on which to float your paints.

Manutex is a finely ground powder often used to thicken screen printing dyes and paints. It also makes an excellent size. Buy it from art shops which specialise in silk screen printing.

To make up approximately 2 litres (2 quarts) of size, pour 100ml (a mug) of lukewarm water into a plastic bucket and slowly sprinkle on two tablespoonsful of the powder, whisking continuously to mix the two together. The mixture should be absolutely smooth: if it isn't, force it through a fine sieve to mash out the lumps.

Slowly add more lukewarm water to bring the quantity up to 2 litres (2 quarts), stirring all the time, and finally whisking to ensure the mixture is completely smooth. Leave overnight at room temperature: don't let it get too cold or it may become very lumpy. If it thickens, add small amounts of lukewarm water until it is the correct consistency again.

Carragheen moss is a seaweed which has been used to make marbling size for centuries, and is still as effective when carefully prepared. Buy it from art and craft shops or health-food stores.

To make 10 litres (10 quarts), pour 8 litres (8 quarts) of water into a large pan and add 150g (5oz) of carragheen moss and a tablespoonful of powdered borax. Bring to the boil and simmer gently, stirring all the time: if the moss is dense and fairly fresh, 4-5 minutes will suffice, but if it is not, continue for longer, until it forms a gluey mass. Hold back a little in case you need it for thickening later, then add 2 litres (2 quarts) of cold water, stir well and leave to cool. If you haven't a large enough pan, make the size up in two batches. When it is cold, pour the mixture through a medium mesh sieve or muslin cloth to get rid of all the solid moss residue. Leave to stand overnight.

If you are not using all the size immediately, it will keep for up to five days if you add 7-8 tablespoons of size preservative before it cools down (this is a 30-35% formaldehyde solution, available from chemists). Cover it and leave in a cool place. If the size thickens while it is standing, add water to thin it down, just before you use it.

When you have prepared the size, pour some

into a small dish. Drop a little paint onto the surface to see whether it floats: if it sinks to the bottom, the size is not the correct consistency. Add some more concentrated size mixture to it and test again, until you get it right.

APPLICATION

1. When you are ready to start work, pour the size mixture into a tray until it is three-quarters full: avoid over-filling the tray, as this will make it difficult to manipulate the fabric.

2. Drop paint onto the surface with a pipette, drop brush or wooden stick. The paint should drop easily: if it is too thick, dilute water-based paints with distilled water, and oil-based paints with turpentine. Use a separate pipette, brush or stick for each colour, and for your first attempts, limit yourself to only two colours.

3. Using a pointed stick or multi-toothed comb, draw the paints into a pattern: experiment with straight lines, swirls or waves – and make notes in your source book to remind yourself of the methods by which you achieved any particularly spectacular results.

4. When you are satisfied with the pattern that you have created, lay your fabric on top of the size, in one movement. Then very carefully lift it off, again in one movement: try to avoid any hesitation in laying the fabric on the size, or when lifting it off, as this can distort your pattern.

5. If you have used oil-based paints, wash the fabric under a running cold tap to remove the excess size, then lay it flat on sheets of newspaper to dry.

Leave water-based paints to dry naturally: don't wash off excess size.

FIXING

Follow the manufacturer's instructions to fix the paints, then wash and press the fabric.

SOLVING PROBLEMS

If the *colour spreads too much* on the size, it is because the paint is too thin. Add more paint from the tube or bottle to your existing colour. If it is still too thin, make up a new batch without diluting the paint.

If *white spots or patches* appear on the fabric after it has been marbled, it may be that air bubbles were trapped between the cloth and size – or the fabric may have been creased. Try again, making sure the fabric has been washed and ironed so that it is absolutely smooth and even, and taking extra care as you lay the fabric on the size.

If the *colour does not spread* or if it *sinks to the bottom*, it may be that it is too thick. Dilute with turpentine for oil-based paints.

Or it may be that a thin film has settled on the surface of the size because it has been left standing uncovered. Skim the film off with a plastic ruler, or lift it off by laying a sheet of thin paper on the size.

If the *paint flakes off* the fabric, it is probably the result of drying it too close to direct heat: on top of a radiator, for instance. Always leave the marbled fabric to dry slowly and naturally, preferably flat.

(*right*) BATHING BEAUTIES
Although bathrooms are often one of the smallest rooms in the house, they are also one of the most important. And it is arguable that the occupants spend more time contemplating the decor than they might in any other room. Your planning needs to combine warmth, comfort and a sense of luxury with plenty of interesting features that are attractive, but not distracting. Colours should be harmonious, to create a relaxing atmosphere, but

not boring: similarly, touches of pattern should please the eye without being irritating or overpowering.

The plain bath towels in the illustration have been given the designer touch with swirling marbled borders in contrasting colours – which are echoed in the appliquéed scallop shells. These were drawn and painted on plain fabric, as described in Chapter 7, before being cut out. Shells appear again on the shelf above, this time in the guise of small

tablets of soap resting on a bed of pot pourri in the marble stoneware bowl. The soaps and dried flower petals combine to scent the bathroom luxuriously.

Bamboo wall shelves and a Victorian towel rail give the room a feeling of natural rustic warmth, softening the strong tones of the wallpaper, towels and floor covering. Interesting pot plants, trailing an abundance of fresh green foliage, are always an attractive bathroom feature

CHAPTER 13

PAINTING FOR THE FESTIVE SEASON

SPECIAL OCCASIONS AND DECORATIONS

At no other time is the home more the focus of attention than when the family gathers to celebrate an important festival. The time of year and the event depends on your own particular faith, of course. But although we have chosen subjects that are traditionally associated with Christmas, fabric painting is the perfect medium to create any kind of symbolic table linen and other special accessories for the home, as well as colourful decorations.

Since families always draw closer at such times, this is a wonderful opportunity for members of every generation to get together around the table with paints or felt-tips – according to age – to produce highly individual cards and gift tags, decorations for the tree, table or mantelpiece – or perhaps even to make their own Christmas stockings!

Paint a piece of Habotai silk with colourful abstract designs using one or more of the special effects methods described in Chapter 6, or outline more conventional subjects with gutta (Chapter 10): then cut the silk into pieces and mount them inside special greetings cards. Your friends can't fail to be impressed! If you prefer to draw and paint (Chapter 7) or stencil (Chapter 9) or create a piece of batik (Chapter 11) to convey your greeting, use a fine cotton like Primissima.

Alternatively, iron your painted fabric onto one side of a sheet of thin white card, cut it into small shapes (rectangles, squares, circles, etc, as you please), punch a hole in one corner to hold a narrow ribbon tie – and you have an artistic, and most unusual, gift tag or Christmas tree decoration. Use Vilene Bondaweb or Wunder Under to join

Hand-painted fabric cards, for the personal touch

130

the two together: this will ensure a very smooth and professional finish, with no frayed edges.

Bleached cotton sheeting makes practical tablecloths and napkins that can be brought out and enjoyed again year after year. The brilliantly intense colours of fabric paints lend themselves so well to decorations of this nature, when you hope to stimulate a cheerful and convivial party mood. And don't forget that you can embellish your brightly painted design still further with touches of additional surface decoration, using a shimmering gutta outliner.

Tiny gifts for your guests can become treasured reminders of a happy occasion when they are presented in special little draw-string bags painted with an appropriate motif, together with the recipient's name, the occasion and the date. Children would be even more delighted with a take-home bag of sweets if it had their name boldly emblazoned on the outside – perhaps further enriched with some gold gutta doodling.

So whether you are celebrating Christmas, Rosh Hashanah, Diwali, a special anniversary or perhaps a family occasion such as a wedding, bar mitzvah or baptism, your fabric paints equip you with the means to make the event even more memorable.

The enchanting holly patterned silk cushion shows how easily batik adapts to a modern setting. Full instructions for making it are given in Chapter 11. The tree decorations and the Christmas stocking are both worked on bleached cotton sheeting, using the drawing and painting technique described in Chapter 7. Deka Permanent paints were used, and further sparkle added with Deka gutta outliners.

SANTA'S CHRISTMAS STOCKING

MATERIALS

50cm (½yd) bleached cotton sheeting, 40cm (16in) wide
50cm (½yd) red Habotai silk, 40cm (16in) wide, to back
50cm (½yd) firm cotton fabric, 80cm (32in) wide, to line
Matching thread
Deka Permanent paints: Red, Blue, Yellow and Black
Deka gutta outliners: Pink and Gold

1. Draw the shape you wish your stocking to be on the cotton sheeting.
2. Draw and paint a freehand design of your own, or follow the example in the photograph. This is patterned with circles of black painted over blue, and a border of blue diamonds above a wavy band of yellow: then the background is filled in with red, leaving a white edge round the circles. Pink and gold gutta outliners were used to decorate the stocking with abstract lines and dots, and to draw miniature Christmas trees inside the motifs. When dry, iron-fix as directed in Chapter 7.
3. Cut the stocking shape out, adding a seam allowance all round.
4. Right sides together, pin the stocking to lining fabric: cut the lining to match and then join the two pieces together along the top edge. Un-pin, turn to the right side, tack and press.
5. Use the stocking as a pattern to cut out another piece of lining fabric. Then cut a piece of red backing fabric and join them together as described for the front (but remember to reverse the shape).
6. Right sides together, join the back and front of the stocking all round the raw edge. Trim and clip the seam, then turn to the right side and press again.

TRADITIONAL CHRISTMAS TREE HANGINGS

To make two each of three designs – as illustrated:

MATERIALS

50cm (½yd) bleached cotton sheeting
50cm (½yd) red Habotai silk (or alternative) to back
1m (1yd) iron-on Vilene or Pellon (single-sided)
50cm (½yd) Vilene Bondaweb or Wunder Under
1.5m (1½yd) fine gold cord or gift-tie
Adhesive tape (optional)
Deka Permanent paints in the colours indicated below
Deka gold gutta outliner

1. Trace and transfer the shapes to your cotton fabric as described in Chapter 4: use a light coloured pencil and leave about 2.5cm (an inch) of spare fabric between them.
2. Following the illustration for guidance, draw, paint, decorate and fix the designs as instructed in Chapter 7. The colours used for the examples in the photograph are as follows:
Trees: Red and Green : Green and Gold
Baubles: Red, Yellow and Gold : Pink (with shine) and Gold
Boxes: Blue, Pink and Gold : Green and Red
3. Back with (single-sided) iron-on Vilene or Pellon.
4. Back the Vilene or Pellon with Bondaweb or Wunder Under.
5. Back the red silk with (single-sided) Vilene or Pellon.
6. Peel the paper backing off the front piece and bond the two pieces together.
7. Cut out all the shapes neatly with sharp scissors round the outer edge.
8. Make loops from 25cm (9in) lengths of cord or gift-tie and fix the cut ends to the back of the decoration with tape. Or make a hole at the top and fix the loop through it, knotting the cut ends.

(*right*)
Tree decorations and Christmas stocking, worked on bleached cotton sheeting, using the drawing and painting technique

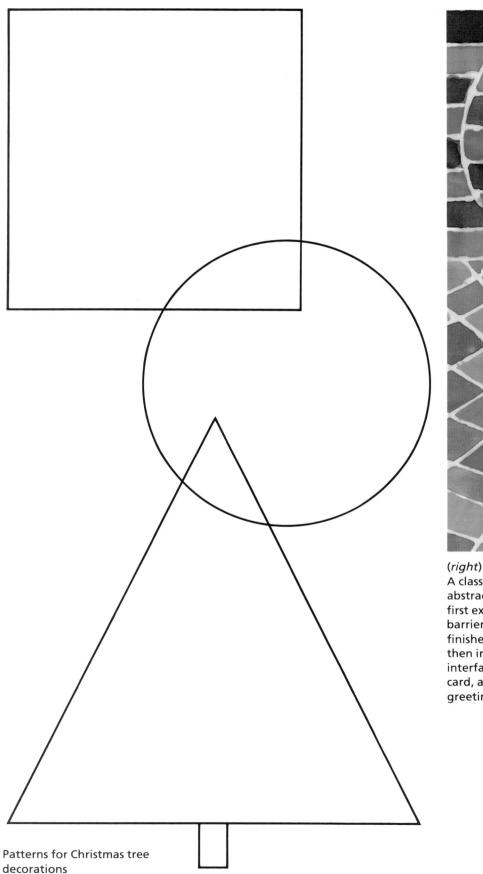

(*right*)
A class of 9-11-year-olds chose abstract geometric designs for their first experiments with gutta resist barriers and glowing silk paints. The finished fabric, as illustrated, was then ironed onto a non-woven interfacing, or bonded directly onto card, and cut up to make colourful greetings cards and gift tags

Patterns for Christmas tree decorations

CHAPTER 14

FABRICS OF ANTIQUITY

Throughout this book it has been impossible to avoid repeatedly remarking on the way fabric painting materials and equipment have developed, improved and changed in a comparatively short period of time. Even now, new products are continually being introduced, superseding existing ones, offering versatile new techniques, or just making the craft even simpler and more trouble-free. This revolution has removed a great deal of the mystique that previously surrounded fabric painting, revealing instead the great potential the craft has to offer, and encouraging a much wider interest in it.

Nevertheless, it is interesting to speculate that the exciting range of easy-to-use products with which we are now tempted only serves to emphasise the problems and difficulties which hindered, and must have frustrated, fabric painters in the past. On reflection, it seems strangely surprising, and all the more admirable, that the craft was so popular amongst amateurs over a hundred years ago. Although professional silk painters had been at work for many centuries, it was those craft-minded people, the Victorians, who developed the art in a new form.

The Industrial Revolution, domestic servants and a new-found affluence presented middle-class Victorian ladies with empty hours to fill. Brought up to believe that a woman's place was in the home – and also that idleness was to be abhorred – nineteenth century ladies and their daughters set to work with their needles, scissors and paintbrushes, eagerly exploring every new craft that appeared on the scene, and developing it to furnish their homes with yet more artistic bric-a-brac.

Fabric painting was one of these, though the technique was a far cry from those described in this book. The basic principle was similar to the drawing and painting method described in Chapter 7. But the paints were thick oil colours, and the fabrics they used were rich velvets and

(*right*)
PAISLEY SHAWL, mid-nineteenth century. The paisley design originated in India, where many different versions were woven, painted or embroidered into shawls for the princesses of the royal courts. Husbands and lovers, returning to the West from trips to India, brought similar shawls home as gifts for their ladies, and by the middle of the nineteenth century they had become an extremely popular fashion, worn over white cotton or silk blouses during the day, and instead of a cape or bolero jacket in the evening. Soon Indian craftsmen were mass-producing the shawls to meet the demand, block printing the intricate designs on cotton and wool in the jewel colours for which their country is famed.

The teardrop shape has been fascinating and inspiring designers for some four hundred years, and is still as popular today. Sit down with a blank teardrop in front of you and see how easy it is to 'doodle' your own paisley design, simply by allowing your pencil to fill it in and decorate the edge with invented flowers and foliage, swirls, scrolls, scallops, dots, dashes and squiggles!

heavy satin. Favourite subjects were, as always, flowers and birds – but perhaps the most popular was fruit. Great bowls and baskets piled high with unbelievably perfect fruit painted on velvet still survive: shiny apples with rosy cheeks; yellow-green pears touched with gold; apricots, peaches, nectarines and bunches of grapes, all with a misty bloom; towering pineapples, dark plums, glowing citrus fruits, fat gooseberries and outsize cherries. Obviously the texture of the fabric suggested the velvet-like skin of a peach to these often highly talented artists, but their exploitation of the medium and representation of the subjects can be quite breathtaking in its realism. This standard of workmanship is all the more impressive when one compares the materials available at that time with the facilities that we have at our fingertips today.

Many paintings from the past still survive, but junk shops are not usually the best place to find them, as all too often they have been neglected, or have not withstood the passing of time, and the damage is past repair. Unfortunately, little or nothing can be done to restore the condition of fabric when it has deteriorated over the years, or been affected by damp and mildew, sunlight or staining. So obviously the best examples will find their way to good antique shops, and their rarity will be reflected in their price.

If you have any examples of nineteenth-century fabric painting in your possession, or are able to purchase any well-preserved pieces, it is important to store them very carefully in a dry

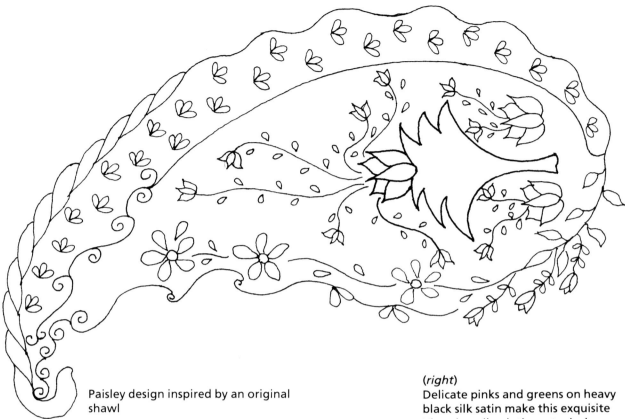

Paisley design inspired by an original shawl

(but not hot) place, between sheets of acid-free tissue paper. The drier the oil paints become, the more they tend to flake and crack, so it is essential to keep them absolutely flat. If you want to display them as pictures, choose a 'box' type frame, so that the glass stands away from the fabric, and doesn't touch it. Be sure to go to a reputable picture-framer, preferably with experience of working with antique textiles, as inferior materials can affect your fabric. And avoid hanging the picture in direct sunlight or over a working fireplace.

OIL PAINTING ON VELVET OR SATIN

Use a good quality *cotton or silk velvet* with a very fine, smooth pile – or a *heavy silk satin,* if you can find one.

Choose your *oil paints* carefully: avoid bright colours in favour of more muted ones that have a slightly faded, antique appearance. The Georgian range of artists' colours has a distinctly authentic Victorian feeling.

(*right*)
Delicate pinks and greens on heavy black silk satin make this exquisite Victorian oil painting a typical example of the craft that was so popular in the mid-nineteenth century. This beautifully preserved piece was the inspiration for the cushion and covered ring binder (overleaf)

Use *turpentine* to dilute the paints and also for cleaning your equipment.

Look for *brushes* with a fairly tough bristle: watercolour brushes with soft bristles are unsuitable.

You will need a flat wooden or plastic *palette* on which to mix your colours.

It is advisable to use a *frame,* the same size as the fabric, together with the necessary *pins,* as described in Chapter 3. Alternatively, use *masking tape,* to avoid damaging the edge of the fabric with pin-marks.

Fill a *jar* with turpentine to keep your brushes moist and clean: but have *another jar* in which to stand them upside-down whilst they are not in use.

Plenty of old *rags* or *paper towels* are needed for cleaning and drying off.

APPLICATION

1. Stretch your fabric over the frame, fixing it with pins or masking tape: make sure it is absolutely smooth, but don't pull it too tight.

2. Trace the design from this page and then transfer it to your fabric, using the most appropriate method described in Chapter 4.

3. Prepare your brushes and paints: moisten the brush with turps and squeeze out the paints that you plan to use onto the palette.

4. Mix the colours, if necessary, then apply the paint to the fabric, building up the layers until the picture is completed to your satisfaction.

5. Remove the fabric from the frame before the paint is completely dry, as this will enable it to settle into the natural tension of the fabric. Leaving the paint to dry out completely on the stretched fabric may cause it to crack.

6. Clean and dry all your equipment and utensils very thoroughly after use, then store in a dry place.

TIGER LILIES CUSHION AND BINDER COVER

Inspired by a real piece of Victorian fabric painting, the artist made use of modern materials and techniques to paint the fabric used to make this attractive cushion, and to cover an ordinary ring binder. Note the interesting juxtapositioning of the design and the contrasting colourways: this is a good example of how the same design can be interpreted in various ways to create totally different effects.

Both the cushion and binder fabric were worked on Primissima cotton: the cushion was backed with silk fabric, and the binder lined with calico. The design (see pattern) was traced onto the fabric (Chapter 4) with a light coloured pencil, to be painted in (Chapter 7) with Deka Permanent paints.

The square cushion may be any size: a plate was used to draw a circle in the centre. Always apply the darkest colours first, working through the deeper ones to the lightest. In this case the black

background was painted before the flowers and foliage. The pale pink background of the centre circle is a mixture of red and white, and the subtle colours and shading of the flowers themselves are all the result of mixing the paints until just the required shade is achieved.

Much brighter colours have been used to cover the ring binder, to illustrate the marked contrast between the same design when it is interpreted in strong colours compared to the pastel shades and sombre black background of the cushion. Deka Permanent cerise and black both work well with the yellow lilies. The random positioning of the lilies also compares with the formal arrangement on the cushion. The backgrounds are reversed too, the ring binder having the black section in the centre, making the dark area much smaller, but at the same time having the effect of throwing the central lily into prominence.

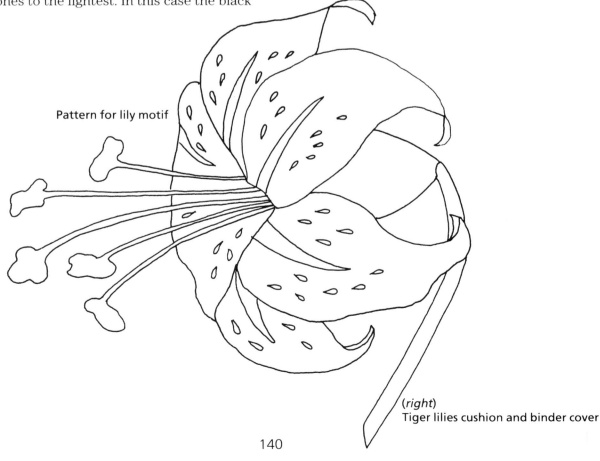

Pattern for lily motif

(right)
Tiger lilies cushion and binder cover

CHAPTER 15

PAINTED PATCHWORK

The basic principle of patchwork must have originated when someone, somewhere, looked at a few bits of precious cloth which were too small to serve any useful purpose – and sewed them together to make one larger piece of fabric that *could* serve a useful purpose! This intensely practical craft is best known in the form of patchwork quilts, painstakingly stitched by resourceful housewives from odd scraps of plain and printed fabric, to become family heirlooms.

Many hours of patient sewing and thousands of tiny stitches went into these serviceable bedcovers, and the results were so colourful and attractive that eventually the patches adopted different geometric shapes which, when stitched together, formed a planned design, instead of being just a collection of small squares joined at random. The pioneer settlers of North America devised the traditional patterns and designs that are now recognised and admired the world over, and which gave the simple patchwork quilt the status of an art form.

The craft of patchwork is as popular as ever. But its character has changed, far removed from its thrifty origins. The patchwork enthusiast no longer hoards and sews together any odd scraps of fabric. The design is carefully planned beforehand and, likely as not, all the fabrics will be specially purchased. Indeed, colour co-ordinated cottons printed with tiny designs are specially produced for just this purpose.

No doubt you are already imagining the opportunities and possibilities offered by your fabric paints! Instead of searching high and low for just the right combination of plain and patterned fabrics, in just the right weight, and just the right colours for the design you visualise – all you have to do is mix the right paints. Or, instead of buying a selection of colour co-ordinated fabrics, all you need is one piece of firm cotton and a tastefully planned colour scheme: the fabric could be either your basic colour – or plain white, enabling you to paint your own backgrounds.

Cut a card template to draw your patchwork shapes – hexagons, pentagons, diamonds, triangles or squares – leaving enough spare fabric around each to turn under the raw edge. Then paint them with tiny patterns of your own design, mixing and matching your colours artistically to merge and tone with the setting in which the finished work will appear. The result will be doubly rewarding – a designer accessory that nevertheless allows you to congratulate yourself on reviving the practical aspect of patchwork.

Once you have begun to cheat in this way, you might be tempted to carry your duplicity still further . . . Why, you may ask yourself, bother to cut the shapes out and sew them all together again? If a busy life prevents you having the time for the patient stitching of our ancestors, why indeed . . . when you can simply paint your patchwork design straight onto a flat piece of fabric. It's cheating shamefully, of course: but who cares, when you can produce something with all the colourful charm of true patchwork – in a fraction of the time that it would take to stitch.

Genuine hexagonal patches were appliquéed onto a plain ground to make the colourful Hedgerow Fruit cushion. But the different shapes which combine to create the Sunburst design were stitched together only in the painter's imagination

PAINTED PATCHWORK CUSHIONS

The two cushions (page 143) demonstrate the versatility of fabric paints, and how cleverly they lend themselves to patchwork cheating! The oblong cushion, attractively decorated with hedgerow fruit, has four 'real' patches, backed with iron-on Vilene or Pellon, joined in a line and then appliquéed along the centre. This may be done by machine, but hand-sewing is much neater, and worth a little extra time and effort.

The design is drawn and painted (Chapter 7) on Primissima cotton using Deka Permanent paints for the patchwork shapes and patterned black borders, and Deka-Silk paint for the plain green background. The method and order of applying the paints is the same as for the tiger lily cushion in the previous chapter, and once again the colour scheme has been reversed, showing cerise berries against a black ground and black berries on cerise.

Using a card template, the patches were outlined on a separate piece of fabric, as described above, then painted and fixed before being cut out with a 1cm (⅜in) seam allowance all round. The patchwork shape was drawn and cut again in Vilene or Pellon and ironed onto the back of the painted fabric, then the surplus fabric was folded neatly over the edge of the backing and tacked all the way round to hold it in place while the patches were sewn together and appliquéed to the plain green fabric. The painted borders were joined on at each side to make this very eye-catching 'designer patchwork' cushion.

The second cushion is totally dishonest, but if deception can produce such exciting results, surely it's excusable! You will recognise the methods used to create this brilliant sunburst of patchwork shapes against a dramatic purple ground suggesting an ominously stormy sky. The 'patches' are all shapes and size: hexagons, pentagons and triangles were outlined in clear gutta on Habotai silk, then filled in with Deka-Silk paints and freely decorated with scrolls using a gold gutta outliner (Chapter 10). The abstract pattern on the purple background is the result of sprinkling the wet paint with coarse sea salt (Chapter 6), to create an illusion of movement that sets off the centre design to perfection.

As a concession to genuine patchwork, the design was machine-stitched along the barrier lines after the paints had been fixed and the fabric washed, but before the cushion was made up.

Patchwork patterns

CHAPTER 16

CREATING A HOME FOR YOUR TEXTILE PAINTING

To show your fabric painting to the very best advantage in the home, you need to create a perfect setting – a background environment which enhances your work, and surroundings which complement it. Your own individual interior will reflect your character as well as suiting your practical needs and budget. But careful planning is necessary to ensure an attractive and, if you want it, a striking result.

The classic styles of romantic bedrooms and quietly elegant sitting and dining rooms have been popular for many decades, initially because most of us want relaxed and comfortable surroundings which help to create a happy mood, whilst not being so obtrusive that one tires of them quickly. But the main reason elegance and romanticism have lasted so long is that the actual aesthetics of the styling is so neutral that one can use them as a basis to express one's own personality and taste. Either situation offers a perfect background to be toned down, or brightened up, to be subtle or dramatic, with the use of a variety of textiles, designs and colours.

This focus on surroundings is particularly relevant in the context of textile painting, when it is essential to achieve a harmonious blend of fabrics and colours for a well-balanced result. There is a wide variety of magazines on the market to help you plan your home in a way that will create the perfect setting for your own textile painting. You can see what is new, fashionable or currently being revived, and absorb ideas.

Study the photographs and notice the background settings which have been chosen to show furniture and fabrics to the best advantage. Consider them carefully, wondering if they would work for *you*. Many shops and manufacturers produce beautifully illustrated catalogues, and these too are full of imaginative new ideas, treatments and colourways to inspire you. Any decorating shop will have a supply of paint shade cards, which are invaluable when you finally come to decide your decor, as they allow you to see in your own home exactly how the paints you choose for walls, woodwork and furniture will mix and match with your fabrics.

Your choice of style will depend on the function of the room you are decorating, the personality and taste of the occupant or occupants, and also the size, shape and aspect. Here are a few suggestions and guidelines to help you create your chosen basic style, whether it be anything from romantic to high tech, in order to achieve the harmonious atmosphere in which the full effect of your fabric painting can be appreciated.

Remember that it is safer to stick to a fairly co-ordinated colour or design scheme if you have limited space, as too much contrast can make a small area look cluttered and confusing. And as *you*, the designer, are creating the patterns – the plainer everything else, the better: competing patterns usually fight to the kill!

ROMANCE IN MANY MOODS

Most of us seek romance somewhere in our everyday lives, and this is reflected in romantic styling of clothing and furnishings – from lovers' knots on wedding dresses to four-poster beds draped with lace! A romantic setting will have natural beauty and harmony, but it can be demure or opulent, as you and your paintbrush wish.

Medium to lightweight fabrics are necessary for the soft, delicate effect which you want to achieve, but curtains and drapes can be lined with a denser, heavier fabric for practical purposes. Festoon blinds and softly draped curtains add volume to window frames: try for a billowy effect which will lend a gentle, even ethereal, feeling of airy lightness.

If you are planning a bedroom, make the bed the focal point. Edge crisp white cotton sheets with lace – to complement a beautifully painted and embroidered quilt or coverlet, or a mass of scatter cushions painted with a dainty pattern and finished with extravagant lace flounces.

Choose dreamy pastels or dusty pastel shades on a softer pastel or white ground. For a clean, crisp effect, nothing is more successful than pure white broderie anglaise or cotton lace. A satin ribbon trimming will incorporate them into your main colour scheme.

Flowers and flounces, bows and buntings . . . all spell romance. Choose an extrovert full-blown rose design, or the dainty freshness of tiny rosebuds; have small sprigs of lavender, a pattern of simple field daisies or sprays of mimosa. Stripes

(*right*) BUTTERFLY BEDROOM
This enchanting room shows fabric painting at its most romantic – and, on a more practical level, at its most versatile. The light and airy atmosphere created by the high, wide window is accentuated and enhanced by the butterfly theme: they hover here, there and everywhere, their soft pastel pink and mauve wings caught in apprehended flight.

Voluminous curtains of soft white muslin are draped across the windows, the hems prettily caught up to break the long drop from the old-fashioned brass curtain rail. Diagonal lines of tiny butterflies flutter across the fabric – miniature version of those that have alighted on the bedspread and pillows.

The simple design lends itself to several techniques: stencils, gutta, batik or drawing and painting would all be equally successful. So choose the method that appeals to you most, or is best suited to the fabrics that you are using.

A small matching rag rug covers the wooden floor beside the bed, and the same colour scheme is followed through in the paper umbrella lampshade, and the wide velvet ribbon bow which supports the two framed silhouette portraits on the plain pinky-mauve wall

(*left*)
Pattern for butterfly design

and geometric designs can work well when properly co-ordinated with softer, less angular patterns: for instance, plain broad pastel stripes overlaid, intertwined or alternating with flowers. Patterned piping or frills on plain cushions, or borders on covers and curtains will create contrast and interest.

THE CHALLENGE OF CHILDREN'S ROOMS

From the age of about seven children usually have quite definite ideas as to what they want from their bedroom, so it is worth sitting down with them to find out what they would like. Then together you can work out how to achieve their demands and requirements.

Here the bed *won't* be the focal point – though it still provides an excellent painting ground for pillow, quilts and covers. But more important to the young occupant will be adequate facilities for work and play, plenty of storage space and a good

area of wall for posters and pictures. The choice of bedroom furniture specifically designed with children in mind ranges from pretty to ultra modern. This enables you to plan a room which will satisfy the child and be practical too.

Once the furniture has been established, let the child choose the theme for the overall styling of the room. But don't forget how fickle children can be: today's obsession may be replaced by an equally passionate, but completely different, enthusiasm tomorrow! So when planning children's rooms, it is even more important than elsewhere to create a neutral background which will be able to cope with a succession of prevailing interests and moods.

If the room is shared, there may be a conflict of ideas. You, as mediator, will have to try to reach a happy compromise! This is yet another situation where a plain and neutral background will help solve the problem. Bunk beds save space, and the rest of the room can be divided or not as the children wish. Desks, tables, bookshelves or

(*left*) Stencilling designs have been used to decorate this light and spacious child's room, suitable for a girl or boy. The walls are painted soft blue with a mottled finish, and a frieze of gaily coloured stencilled ducks sets the design-theme. The same mix of bright colours is repeated for the toy stencils which decorate the white-painted bed, chest of drawers, toy chest and shelves – and these stencils have been used for the crisp white cotton bedlinen too. The neutral colour of the sturdy wall-to-wall floor covering works perfectly as an unobtrusive surround to the stencilled rug (*picture courtesy of Caroline Warrender*)

cupboards may be positioned to give each child their own space, so that different tastes and interests can be kept separate and personal. It isn't always easy, but it *can* be done – especially if the children themselves have been consulted, and feel they have planned the room between them (and just commissioned you to do the work). Remember that at this age, although they need a guiding hand, children have a tremendous creative ability, because they are so totally uninhibited and haven't yet learned that it is possible to make mistakes.

Needless to say, all the furnishings must be sturdy and hard-wearing. Choose co-ordinated fabrics, wallpaper or paint, and floor covering. Bed linen and covers, curtains, cushions and toy bags offer ample material for painting your own interpretations of the child's favourite subjects, and rugs could be stencilled to match.

TRADITION FOR THE NURSERY

Nursery colour-schemes have always focussed on soft pastels. The old fashioned rules of pale blue for a boy and pink for a little girl have been broken to allow lemon, lavender and pale tangerine a place in the paint charts. But although stronger colours, like navy blue or brown, have become popular in recent years, the designs are always very dainty, and muted by a white background.

This concentration on soft shades is not only because there is something very sentimental about a new baby, which demands pretty surroundings and a romantic setting: the baby itself prefers calm, quiet pastels to bright colours and hectic designs.

Once again a neutral background, in either white or whatever pastel shade you choose, will allow you to use your paintbrush on curtains, cradle drapes, pillows, coverlets, patchwork quilts, cushions, lampshades, rugs . . . and all those necessary bits and bobs of baby equipment like towelling capes, changing sheets, carry-cots or baby-nests, travel holdalls and so on.

The choice of design must be your own, and will reflect your personal taste in these matters. It might be anything from traditional nursery rhyme characters to any simple abstract shape, like a button mushroom or the baby's initial, repeated at random all over the fabric.

HIGH TECH IN TOMORROW'S WORLD

The advance of technology has made itself felt in the home quite as much as anywhere else. Domestic chores have been eased or even eradicated by machines and gadgets, and our houses are equipped with television sets, hi-fi units and computer software. Almost always the pieces of furniture which represent this new lifestyle are streamlined, and in many cases very attractive. As a result, there is a whole new field of interior design to explore, which offers exciting opportunities to reflect your own personality and outlook in a setting which looks to the future, rather than echoing the past.

Look for glazed cottons and other shiny materials which will make the overall appearance smooth and stylish. Leather also works well, whilst rugs are not only ideal for the floor, but make a wonderful wall decoration too. Counteract cold materials, like steel and chrome, and soften straight lines and hard angles with strongly textured fabrics which emphasise warmth and comfort.

Black is a favourite base tone and, if used correctly, can give an exciting background for your painting. Striking contrasts can be created by combining black with primary colours such as bright yellow and blue accompanied by white. To tone down the dominant black, use pastels and other shades which soften the general appearance, without detracting from the dramatic effect of the black base tone.

As the style itself is composed of sharp angular lines and clever streamlining, textile patterns must blend in. Work with bold geometric and striped designs – or if you prefer a floral theme, your blooms will need to reflect the dominant mood of clarity, simplicity and contrast.

An interesting theme might be to echo carefully chosen ceramics on your upholstery, curtains and linen. Fabric painting opens up realms of fantasy, making it possible to add a unique and individual note of co-ordination – like the example shown opposite.

COLOUR IN THE HOME

When it comes to deciding the colour scheme for a room, you have to be sure that the colours you choose are going to work hard for you. They will create the landscape into which you set your painted textiles: so they must do their job properly and provide a background which enhances and displays them to the greatest advantage. Just remember the importance of the frame and mount in displaying a picture: your work is the picture – mounted and framed by the room which surrounds it.

Overwhelmed by an array of competing shade cards, you will probably be shocked at the range of decorating possibilities that they offer. It is tempting to be carried away on a wave of enthusiasm for an enchanting colour scheme which, delightful as it may be in the brochure, does nothing for the textiles you have worked so hard to design and paint. So make sure that *they* are the focal point of your consideration when visualising the room they will occupy, and allow *them* to be the persuasive element in dictating your choice of background colours.

Variations on the high-tech design

(*right*) HIGH TECH
If you are setting out to make an impact, it is important that the impression you create shows that you have style and flair. Strong, bold colour schemes should reflect your own personality. Your decor will be making a statement about *you*: it should say emphatically that you are assertive and self-assured. So it's important to get it right!

A combination of bright colours dramatised by black should make the impact you want. But they need to be very carefully thought out, always remembering that you are planning a home: so your choice must create a warm and welcoming atmosphere too.

The colour scheme in this room hits exactly the right note. All the dramatic impact is there – but the hard lines, sombre black and cool blue-greens are relieved by warm pinks and softened by the curves of the vase and wall light and the plump cushions.

The Roman blind is bordered by the geometric design that covers the hand-painted sofa, whilst its bright colours suggest sunlight beyond, even if there is none. And there is sunshine too, as well as a touch of humour, in the giant sunflowers, which make the room friendly and inviting

Ultimately, the colours you choose must be suited to your own personal tastes and environment. The range of styles described in the first part of this chapter should have helped you to decide which is the one for you, and given you a clear picture of the atmosphere and mood you wish to create. And of course, the textiles you have designed will obviously be very much a reflection of your own personality. So your canvas is already far from bare: you know the *kind* of room you want . . . and you can see what you want to display in it. All you need now is the right choice of base tones.

CHOOSING THE RIGHT BASE TONES

As you will have gathered, a 'base tone' is simply the basic tone on which you structure the rest of your colour scheme. Generally, they will be your walls, carpets, curtains and paintwork. You can choose one, two or three: but never have more than three, as too many layers of colour will kill the effect you are aiming to create.

For instance, suppose you have chosen a warm peach base tone for your living room, with perhaps a cream tone to soften it out slightly: you might use these for the walls, curtains and paintwork. Your third choice of colour layering – for the carpet – must be a careful decision. You will want a practical colour, and one that gives a definite feel to the room setting as a whole. But it must be complementary to the peach and cream on which you are building: neither dominating nor distracting.

Peach and cream base tones can be layered with other soft tones, such as warm blues and greens, and grey works well, too. But avoid harsh pinks and reds, as these will distract the eye so much that they become the dominant colour, smothering the gentle subtlety of the peach tone and the softening effect of the cream.

If blue is your choice of base tone, take care that it is well balanced. Although it can be a superb colour with which to work, it is all too easy to turn a room with great potential into a cold and uninviting interior by using blue in the wrong context. Whatever shade of blue you choose, make sure it has enough depth of colour to form a proper base tone. Washed-out blues will just fade away when confronted with another base tone. But a definite blue, combined with yellow or red, can evoke the atmosphere of an impressionist painting – or create the soothing peace of an oasis.

Red and yellow are both colours which need careful thought when used for base toning. There are so many different shades and tints from which to choose that it is important to work out exactly the effect you wish to create, in order to pick the base tone which will best achieve it. Once you have decided the particular yellow or red which will do that job, the colour layers to complete your scheme should suggest themselves and fall into place more easily.

The selection of rooms illustrated in this book shows a variety of colour combinations and schemes, each carefully chosen to ensure the painted designs are shown in the most appropriate or spectacular way. Study and use these, if you need inspiration or guidance. Note how often a subtle or neutral choice of base tones sets off a colourful design: remember, the object of the exercise is to display your fabric painting in a setting where it will achieve its true worth, and be fully appreciated by everyone who visits your home!

WORKSHOP REFERENCE SECTION

FABRICS, PAINTS AND EQUIPMENT

Fabric painting for the home calls for a considerable amount of careful planning and clear thinking. If you are painting on fabric purely for the pleasure of the craft, you have simply to decide the technique you want to employ – which, in turn, will determine the most suitable paints and fabric. But practical factors have to be the primary consideration when textiles are to have a functional purpose, and the technique becomes secondary to the fabric itself.

If you have already planned your design, and decided the technique you wish to use for the article you have in mind, you may find it necessary to alter or adjust either or both. But some kind of compromise is usually possible without changing your original concept too radically. The important thing is to approach the problem from the right direction – and to think it through before you allow yourself to pick up your purse and set out on a serious shopping trip. You may find it helpful to do a little preliminary research to see and feel the kind of fabrics that are available: but at this stage, leave your cheque book at home!

WORKING FABRICS

The range of furnishing fabrics is wide and varied: your choice will be determined by the article you are making and its place in the home. Cushions, curtains, upholstery and table linen all need specific fabrics, as do accessories for the kitchen or bathroom. So your first thoughts must be in this context, remembering the kind of work that the item will have to do. If you are planning curtains, how heavy should they be? Is appearance all that matters – or is warmth a necessary consideration, too? Weight and thickness are very important in choosing curtain fabrics. And will they have to 'fit in' with other furnishings: upholstered chairs and sofas, carpets or rugs? This will affect both the colour and texture of the fabric you choose.

Similar considerations apply to everything you make for the home. Armchairs and sofas call for a tough, durable fabric; scatter cushions don't have to stand up to quite such hard wear; bedspreads can usually be made from a medium to lightweight fabric (though this depends on the occupant of the bedroom!). Always the decision as to which fabric is most suitable for the purpose must come first: fine muslin for sheer curtains, closely woven linen for the table, washable cottons for the kitchen, hard-wearing and cheerful for children's room, soft and gentle for a nursery, towelling for the bathroom.

TWO-WAY COLOUR SCHEMING

Once a decision as to the type of fabric has been made, your next train of thought will inevitably be the colour it should be. You may well have this already in mind, but it is important to think twice before making a firm decision.

Your choice of colour should not only complement, blend or merge with the colour scheme of the room, it must set off your painting to the best advantage, too. It could be that a neutral fabric will be more suitable than a toning shade, letting your painted design pick up the dominant colours of the room instead.

Remember, too, that the paint colours will not be true to the colour chart when used on a coloured background, so you will either have to do some careful mixing or possibly use the type of paint specially prepared for use on darker fabrics.

KEEPING A CLEAR HEAD

It is usually helpful to organise your thinking by making a list of the various points you will need to look for. One's mind is usually much clearer at home, looking at the space one wants to fill, than it is when faced with a bewildering variety of possible fabrics in a large department store. Too often the result can either be a disastrous choice – or to return home down-hearted and empty-handed.

Just jot down the important factors you need to bear in mind: thickness, weight, texture and colour – noting any additional thoughts that have occurred to you whilst you have been considering these points. Most important is a reminder of how practical the fabric needs to be. Dining and sitting rooms require durable fabrics which will combat hard wear – especially if there is a young family around: sticky fingers and muddy paws are a hazard that must be taken into account. Would it be advisable to look for a fabric which will stand frequent washing? Dry-cleaning can become expensive if it happens too often. And if you've decided on something washable, would a non-iron fabric be a good idea – for a child's room, for instance? If you decide on this option, you will need to test a piece of the fabric first, to see how well it takes the paint. Easy-care fabrics are produced by blending a considerable proportion of man-made fibres with the natural ones: and synthetic fabrics are not always sympathetic to textile paints.

Having it all written down in black and white is a good insurance against the possibility of being overwhelmed by too much and too many . . . and also avoids the danger of being carried away by something quite lovely – but totally unsuitable!

If the decision already sounds daunting, don't worry: there is no need for it to be. The following pages describe the variety of fabrics that are suitable for painting – from amongst which you should be able to single out those that will also be suitable for the purpose you have in mind. Note these on your list, and you will have a clear indication of the type of fabric to look for – to guide you in the right direction when you set out to find it.

THE LURE OF SILK

Because of its unique characteristics, silk is the most rewarding fabric on which to paint. It combines the qualities of strength and weight with fine texture and lustre, at the same time absorbing and enhancing the colours of the silk paints to create a clear, translucent radiance.

Silk itself is obtained from the cocoon of the silk worm. This is the fibrous covering that the worm spins around itself as protection when it reaches the chrysalis stage, prior to becoming a silk moth. The cocoons that surrounded the pupating larvae are soaked and hot air dried to remove gummy resin. Then the silk is reeled in very much the same way as it was when Empress See-Ling-Chi invented the reeling machine in 2600 BC – when the Chinese silk industry had already been well established for several hundred years. Today China is second only to Japan as the world's largest producer of silk. Cultivated silk worms produce a fine, even thread, but the wild silk moth caterpillar spins silk of an uneven thickness, which makes the characteristic 'slub' in the weave of wild silk.

The Chinese have been painting on silk for as long as they have been producing it, and textile artists have never ceased to be fascinated by the art. However, there are many different types of silk, determined by their composition. The difference between the most superior and lower quality fabrics is considerable, and is reflected in their price and availability.

Natural silk can vary considerably in colour, ranging from pure white through to shades of ivory, cream, yellow, orange, brown and silver: a pure white effect is often achieved by bleaching. If you are working with a natural coloured silk, always experiment on a spare scrap of the fabric to see how the paint will look on it, as it may well be quite different from the result on a pure white background.

Although silk has always been regarded as fragile and delicate, it is the strongest of all natural fabrics – which means that it can often be ideal for home furnishings. But always check to see whether it can be hand or machine washed, or whether it needs to be dry-cleaned.

PREPARATION AND TREATMENT OF SILK

It is always wise to wash silk before painting, in order to remove any special finishes used by the manufacturer to improve the appearance. Silk will only shrink if it is mixed with cotton or wool fibres. Either wash by hand or dry-clean (but check the manufacturer's instructions first before dry-cleaning).

Washing: Hand-wash silk in lukewarm water, using a very mild detergent specially made for delicate fabrics. Keep it moving in the bowl and rinse very thoroughly with plenty of lukewarm or cold clear water. Never wring silk, as this will damage the filaments and cause it to crease: such creases are almost impossible to remove. Don't tumble-dry either. Roll in a clean towel to remove excess water, then pull the fabric into shape and hang it up to dry naturally.

Ironing: Iron the silk while it is still damp (but not wet, as this may leave unsightly patches): if it is too dry, use a damp cloth. Check that your iron is on the correct setting for silk: it should be warm, not hot. If using a steam iron, cover the silk with a clean, dry cloth.

Storing: Keep silk separate from other fabrics. Wrap it in acid-free tissue paper, or hang it in a polythene bag, in a dry place, away from strong light.

A SELECTION OF SILKS SUITABLE FOR PAINTING

SPUN SILK 120 (AND SPUN SILK 30103) Somewhat similar to a very good cotton lawn. The smooth finish and dense texture means it is delightful to work with, though the high quality makes it expensive. Spun silk 30103 is slightly smoother and lighter weight than 120.

Suitable for: brushwork: sponging: drawing and painting: stencilling: marbling

SILK NOILE Usually a heavier weight fabric. The attractive rough surface texture, and small brown flecks that appear in the cloth, are the result of leftover cocoons and other silk waste becoming mixed in with the spun silk.

Suitable for: brushwork: sponging: drawing and painting: stencilling: marbling

CRÊPE DE CHINE A high quality, lightweight and evenly woven fabric with a smooth surface: it has exceptional draping qualities. Regarded as one of the best silks available, it is expensive, and mainly used by dress designers. However, it may also be used for soft furnishing projects – especially lampshades and cushions.

Suitable for: brushwork: salt: gutta: batik: marbling

HABUTAI Also known as Pongée, and sometimes Jap silk, this hard-wearing shiny fabric is often sold in department stores as lining silk. Its reasonable price and smooth surface make it an ideal medium for the fabric painter. Habutai is available in three weights: 12mm, 8mm and 5mm – 12mm is the heaviest, whilst 5mm is fine and sheer.

Suitable for: salt: brushwork: sponging: drawing and painting: spray stencilling: gutta: batik: marbling

SILK ANTUNG A beautifully textured, fine to medium weight silk with a high sheen and close grain, which is quite rough to the touch. Available in natural ivory and white.

Suitable for: salt: sponging: drawing and painting: gutta: batik: marbling

SILK TWILL A fine to medium weight fabric with a diagonal cross surface grain, which may feel quite rough.

Suitable for: salt: brushwork: sponging: drawing and painting: stencilling: gutta: batik: marbling

DOUPION SILK Lightweight and with a high sheen, this luxurious silk has a bobbly textured surface.

Suitable for: salt: brushwork: sponging: drawing and painting: stencilling

TAFFETA One of the most luxurious silk fabrics, renowned for its paper-like quality. Taffeta comes in several weights, but the ultra smooth surface texture always remains the same.

Suitable for: salt: brushwork: drawing and painting: stencilling: gutta: batik: marbling

SILK MIXTURES There are many available, combining silk with cotton or wool to produce fabrics of varying weights, surface texture and price. These may well be suitable for painting, but test a small piece first, to check the result.

THE FRESHNESS OF COTTON

All through history cotton has been the commonsense fabric of the people, used by all levels of society for clothing, household linen, soft furnishings and upholstery. Crisp and attractive in appearance, it has all the practical qualities of a hard-wearing, sturdy fabric that can be boiled if necessary, and is easy to cut, sew and dye. All this has made it the world's leading textile.

The Egyptians were producing cotton in 8000 BC, spinning, weaving and dyeing it to make cloth. However, as the cotton industry developed,

Barbados cultivated a strain of the *Gossypium* or cotton plant which produced the best quality fabric, known as 'Sea Island' cotton. This variety was introduced to the United States of America, where the quality was improved still more. Climate, soil and the genes in the *Gossypium* seed all help to determine the quality of the fabric produced.

Cotton reacts well to dyes and paints of all kinds: add to this its practical nature and versatility, and you have an excellent fabric for painting. However, the paints and techniques differ from those employed when working with silk – so the finished effects are quite different, too.

Good quality cotton is not cheap, and can compare with certain types of silk. You may also find that you have to search for pure cottons, as many manufacturers mix cotton with other fibres in order to make the fabric easier to handle, wash and care for.

PREPARATION AND TREATMENT OF COTTON

Most cottons have some kind of finish to emphasise their fresh, new appearance, so you should always wash them first, as this substance may prevent the paint either being absorbed or adhering properly. If the fabric has been pre-shrunk, wash in clear lukewarm water. Cottons that have not been pre-shrunk should be washed at a high temperature with or without detergent before use.

Washing: Most cotton fabrics can be washed at a high temperature, or boiled, using your regular detergent. However, when cotton is mixed with silk or wool, you may have to take special precautions, washing as you would all-silk or all-wool.

Drying: Using a tumble-dryer can cause creasing which is difficult to remove. It can also increase shrinkage. Don't dry in direct sunlight.

Ironing: Pure cotton tends to crease easily. Iron it whilst still damp, or use a steam iron. Pressing under a damp cloth will also remove creases.

NOTE: Don't use a steam iron or damp cloth on cotton or any other kind of fabric before the paints have been fixed.

A SELECTION OF COTTONS SUITABLE FOR PAINTING

PRIMISSIMA A lightweight cotton with a fairly smooth texture.
Suitable for: brushwork: sponging: drawing and painting: stencilling: batik: marbling

VOILISSIMA A lightweight cotton with a softer and smoother texture.
Suitable for: brushwork: sponging: drawing and painting: stencilling: batik: marbling

CAMBRIC AND LAWN Two very lightweight cottons, both extremely soft and smooth in texture, though lawn is slightly shinier and finer than cambric.
Suitable for: salt: brushwork: sponging: batik: marbling

NATURAL SHEETING OR CALICO COTTON Heavyweight white or oatmeal coloured (unbleached) cotton with a medium texture, very tough and durable.
Suitable for: brushwork: sponging: drawing and painting: stencilling

MUSLIN A very sheer and lightweight cotton with a smooth texture and open weave – excellent for net curtaining or summer drapes.
Suitable for: brushwork: sponging: drawing and painting: stencilling: marbling

COTTON POPLIN A smooth, soft textured cotton available in different weights: fairly light, medium and a little heavier.
Suitable for: brushwork: sponging: drawing and painting: stencilling: marbling

COTTON AND SILK OR WOOL MIXTURES Such fabrics are available in various weights, ranging from very fine to medium and heavy. And in both smooth and rough textures, depending on the amount of cotton and silk or wool used, and the method of weaving.

MAN-MADE AND OTHER FIBRES MIXED WITH COTTON These fabrics are very popular, since they are easy to care for and require the minimum of washing and drying time. However, some do not respond well to fabric paints, so it is important to try out your paints on a small piece of the fabric to see how they take – and also to wash it in order to check the colour fastness.

THE NATURAL APPEAL OF LINEN AND THE WARMTH OF WOOL

LINEN A superior cloth made from flax, which can

range from light through medium to heavyweight. It almost always has a very smooth texture with a slight sheen, and a visible weave or grain. Linen creases very badly, but this characteristic is considered part of its charm. It is advisable to experiment on a cheaper fabric with similar properties before embarking on a major project, since linen itself tends to be very expensive.

Suitable for: brushwork: sponging: drawing and painting: stencilling: marbling

NUNSVEILING (LAMBSWOOL) A medium weight woven fabric with a fine and soft texture, which lends itself to a variety of soft furnishings.

Suitable for: salt: brushwork: sponging: drawing and painting: gutta: marbling

WOOL TWILL A medium weight fabric that can be made out of various wools: it has a diagonal cross weave.

Suitable for: brushwork: sponging: drawing and painting: stencilling: marbling

VARIOUS OTHER WOVEN WOOLLENS are suitable for painting, so it is worth experimenting with any that appeal to you, or suggest themselves for the soft furnishing you require. Remember that wool, like silk, needs special treatment: follow the previous instructions for washing and care of silk.

Note: Never tumble dry.

WHICH FABRIC FOR WHAT PURPOSE?

The following suggestions are only for guidance, and the ultimate choice will obviously depend on your judgement for the type of soft furnishings you require, bearing in mind the advice at the beginning of this section. For instance, bedroom curtains will generally be a lighter weight than those for a sitting room – and linen for a cradle or small child's bed will be finer than your own.

CURTAINS Medium to heavyweight fabrics – closely woven for warmth, if they are not to be lined.

NET CURTAINS Sheer and very lightweight washable fabrics.

UPHOLSTERY Heavy to medium weight, hard-wearing fabrics.

TABLECLOTHS Medium to lightweight, easily laundered fabrics.

TOWELS Light to medium weight cotton towelling.

BED LINEN Medium to lightweight cotton sheeting or easy-care cotton.

ROLLERBLINDS Fabric must be treated with a special finish to ensure stiffness.

PAINTS AND EQUIPMENT

In recent years, as the popularity of fabric painting has grown, a wide variety of paints and allied equipment has appeared on the market. The introduction of improved and easier-to-use products has in turn helped to make the craft even more popular. However, this happy situation means that the range of competing materials tends to make the choice a little bewildering for the inexperienced beginner. The ideal is to experiment with everything that looks interesting, so that you can draw your own conclusions. However, this is not always practical, and also means that you will be left with a lot of quite expensive paints that you will never use again.

Bear in mind that the colour and consistency of different brands of paint will vary from manufacturer to manufacturer. It is wise to avoid mixing different makes, as this can produce streaked or patchy results. If you *are* anxious to mix two different paints, you can tell how successful the result will be by watching how well they amalgamate. If they bind together without much stirring, and remain as one unit, the combination might work. But if the paints separate, there is no point in trying to work with them.

The other important factor that you will wish to consider is the method of fixing the paint. This can vary from simple iron fixing to special fixing solution baths and complicated steaming methods. Once again, the decision is yours: but iron fixing is so quick and trouble-free that this would seem the obvious choice for most beginners. So remember to check the fixing instructions before buying your paints.

To help you find the paints that will suit you and your purpose best, the following is an indication of the major manufacturers and the brands of paint and other products that they produce, together with a description of each type, and details of the purposes to which it is most suited. This should not deter you from exploring the possibilities for yourself, and looking for new or interesting products. But it should make your initial planning a little easier.

DEKA TEXTILE PAINTS This German manufacturer has studied the requirements of modern fabric painters in order to produce a wide selection of paints and dyes that are very easy to use. The range of choice and clear, detailed instructions has made Deka one of the most popular brand names for fabric painting. They are fixed either by ironing, oven baking or in a fixing bath, after which the colours are extremely fast and fade resistant. All products from the entire range can be either machine washed or dry-cleaned.

DEKA SILK SERIES Specifically designed for silk painting techniques, these paints may also be used on other fabrics, such as cotton, wool or man-made fibres: however, the effect is opaque on other fabrics, compared to the translucence of the paints when they are used on silk. There are eighteen colours in the range, plus a white medium 797, that can be added to the colours to produce pastel shades.

DEKA PERMANENT This range consists of nineteen basic and nine metallic shades, designed for painting, stencilling and spraying on all natural fabrics. The paints are fully intermixable, and can be diluted with water. For pastel shades, add 'colourless 400'. If you are painting on a coloured background, always do a test sample first to check the effect, as these paints are fairly transparent.

DEKA FLUORESCENT Six vivid fluorescent colours for painting or printing onto any light coloured fabric.

DEKA 'DECK' COLOURS Twelve opaque colours, including white, especially made for painting on dark coloured backgrounds. May be used on silk, cotton or synthetic fabrics.

DEKA IRON ON A useful technique for children, because there is no mess or danger of spoiling the fabric, either by mistakes or accidental spills. However, this method is only effective on synthetic fabrics, or those with a high synthetic fibre content. The design is first painted on a sheet of paper: the sheet is then placed face down on the fabric and ironed for five minutes. When the paper is removed, the design will be printed permanently on the fabric. The paper 'transfer' may be used several times.

DEKA SILK OUTLINERS Available in ten colours, including gold and silver, plus a clear gutta outliner that can be washed out in lukewarm water after the paints have been fixed. Although the coloured gutta outliners are soluble in water, they can be permanently fixed by ironing on the reverse side of the fabric for about three minutes, after which they are fully washable.

Note: All Deka products are solvent free.

DUPONT TEXTILE PAINTS The French firm of Dupont is renowned for an excellent range of silk paints that may also be used on wool. However, as they actually dye the cloth, steam fixing is necessary to develop the colours, deepening and strengthening the shade, and to fix the paints permanently.

DUPONT SERTI OUTLINERS The Dupont serti outliner does exactly the same job as the Deka gutta outliner, but the coloured ones are only available in a petroleum base. It is essential to work in a well ventilated area, as the fumes can cause nausea or drowsiness, and to remember at all times that the outliner is highly inflammable. Not recommended for use by children, unless under strict supervision. The coloured outliners can only be fixed by steam. The clear serti outliners is now available as a non-solvent barrier fluid.

DUPONT DILUTANT AND CONCENTRATED DILUTANT A medium that may be used to soften the strength of colour in Dupont paints, and also to add volume.

ESSENCE F After a period of time, the petroleum-based serti outliner becomes very sticky. This thinning agent will overcome the problem.

DUPONT ANTI-FUSANT For use with Dupont silk paints, the anti-fusant inhibits the flow of paint. After painting the liquid onto the stretched silk, the colour can be controlled without a serti resist barrier.

EPAISSISANT A substance to thicken colours so that designs may be painted on silk without the use of a serti barrier, or pre-treating the fabric with anti-fusant. Use 20% Epaississant to 80% colour.

OTHER BRANDS OF FABRIC PAINT In addition to the products listed above there is a very wide selection of excellent products available for a variety of purposes. Just remember to follow the manufacturer's instructions very carefully and, if necessary, seek the advice of your art and craft materials supplier.

FABRIC MARKERS, WAX CRAYONS AND TRANSFER PAINTS

Textile markers look just like regular felt-tip pens, and the crayons resemble ordinary wax crayons for use on paper. However, when applied to fabrics, and iron-fixed, they are as permanent as any textile paint. The markers and crayons are suitable for a wide variety of projects, and make an excellent introduction to the craft of fabric painting. And of course, they are so clean and easy to use that they are ideal for children.

There are several brands on the market. Specially recommended are:

DEKA MARKERS : SETASKRIB MARKERS : DYLON MARKERS : PELIKAN MARKERS

Also useful for children's work are the special paints which are applied to paper and then ironed onto the fabric, as described in Chapter 5.

DYES AND DYEING

In some circumstances, such as batik, you may wish to dye the fabric, rather than paint it. There is a good range of dyes available, but it is worth studying them carefully before making your choice, as some are considerably easier to use than others.

DEKA-L AND DEKA 'AKTUELL' Deka-L dyes are available in thirty-three intermixable shades, and 'Aktuell' in twenty-four brilliant colours: they will dye any fabric, including synthetics, and are extremely colour fast. Equally suitable for machine dyeing or for hand dyeing silk and wool.

DYLON COLD WATER DYES Available in twenty-five bright colours that are fast to washing and light, they will dye cotton, linen, silk, viscose, rayon and wool. Use one sachet of DYLON COLD FIX to each tin of dye to make the colour permanent.

GENERAL PREPARATION AND NOTES ON DYEING

Make sure you have plenty of space to work in, especially when dyeing by hand. You will need several large pails or other receptacles for cold dyeing, and large pans for heat dyeing.

Protect any furniture and floor covering with plastic sheeting or newspapers, and wear an apron or old clothing. Remember that dye, even before fixing, usually leaves a permanent stain whenever it comes into contact with textiles. Work in a well ventilated area and wear rubber gloves at all times.

If possible use enamel-lined pans when boiling dyes, as aluminium may have a chemical reaction on the dye, and have a wooden spoon or stick for stirring.

Some products have a fixing solution that is added to the dye, so that fixing takes place whilst the cloth is being dyed. Others require a separate solution to be made up, to which the cloth is transferred from the dye bath. The manufacturer's instructions will make it clear which method is employed.

Afterwards, rinse the fabric in plenty of cool water until all the residue has been removed.

FIXING METHODS AND EQUIPMENT

IRON FIXING Easily the simplest method. When the painting is completed, the fabric is left until it is completely dry (a hand-held hair dryer may be used, with care, to speed the process). Then it is ironed on the reverse side for three to five minutes. Cover very delicate fabrics with a clean cloth before ironing. Always set the iron as high as the fabric allows, as it is the intensity of the heat that fixes the paints.

OVEN BAKING As long as the temperature instructions are correctly followed, this method is quite easy too. Fold the fabric lightly and place it on a baking tray, either carefully covered with, or wrapped in, a sheet of cooking foil. Place on the middle shelf of the oven, and bake for the appropriate length of time. (Take great care to keep the fabric well away from the naked flame in a gas oven.)

STEAM FIXING Special care is needed when following this method, since it is possible to turn a lovely painting into a tragic disaster!

First prepare your fabric by rolling it up in a sheet of greaseproof paper or foil: seal all the edges very carefully, to prevent any moisture, formed by the steam, finding its way inside. Having done this, there are several ways to steam the 'package'.

High Pressure Cooker See the paint manufacturer's instructions for timing.

Steamer Box This may be used on the hob of a conventional cooker.

Uhlig Steamer An upright steamer for professional fabric painters or those planning to take up the craft seriously. The steamer is an expensive piece of equipment, so do make sure you will be getting full value from it before deciding to purchase one! Some suppliers will steam your painted fabric for you, charging per metre for the service.

FIXATIVE BATHS There are several types of fixing solutions on the market. Some are made to be used in conjunction with specific paints: others are designed for individual fabrics – wool, silk or cotton. Follow the manufacturer's instructions.

INDEX